Dreams of Carol Lee

Dan,

God's Grace and Blessings be with you always

E

Dreams of Carol Lee

Edward J. Sekula, Jr.

Copyright © 2011 by Edward J. Sekula, Jr.

Library of Congress Control Number: 2011905099
ISBN: Hardcover 978-1-4568-9781-9
Softcover 978-1-4568-9780-2
Ebook 978-1-4568-9782-6

All rights reserved. No part of this book may be reproduced or transmitted in any form or by any means, electronic or mechanical, including photocopying, recording, or by any information storage and retrieval system, without permission in writing from the copyright owner.

This book was printed in the United States of America.

To order additional copies of this book, contact:
Xlibris Corporation
1-888-795-4274
www.Xlibris.com
Orders@Xlibris.com
90129

CONTENTS

Introduction 13
Dream Interpretation 17
Dream List 21
Dreams In The Bible 23
My Dreams 31
Eulogy: In Memory of Carol Lee 34
My First Dream Of Carol Lee From Heaven 36
Dream # 2—A Picture of Heaven 38
Dream # 3—"Pooky" 40
Dream # 4—Walking in the Presence of God 41
Dream # 5—"Her Rock" 43
Dream # 6—Life in Heaven is Easy and Fun 45
Dream # 7—Fishing in Heaven 47
Dream # 8—Watching Over Me—I 49
Dream # 9—Watching TV Together 52
Dream # 10—Seeing Carol Lee 53
Dream # 11—Last Kiss 54
Dream # 12—Crystal Ice Cave 55
Dream # 13—Fishing Trip 57
Dream # 14—Losing Carol Lee—Again 59
Dream # 15—A "Treatser" 60
Dream # 16—Carol Lee Calling 61
Dream # 17—Working 62
Dream # 18—Remembering 63

Dream # 19—The Conference 65
Dream # 20—Return to Life—Happiness Is Holding Hands 66
Dream # 21—Our Dream Wedding 68
Dream # 22—A Tremendous Cook 70
Dream # 23—Our First Meeting 72
Dream # 24—Eagle Scout Project 75
Dream # 25—Carol Lee's Surprise 77
Dream # 26—Freedom and Happiness 79
Dream # 27—Trout Fishing 81
Dream # 28—Walking on Water 84
Dream # 29—Bird Costume 86
Dream # 30—Watching Over Me—II 88
Dream # 31—Advice on How to Help Someone 89
Dream # 32—Two New Puppies 91
Dream # 33—Marching Band Competition 93
Dream # 34—Meeting in Heaven 95
Dream # 35—Falling Asleep at the Wheel 97
Dream # 36—Searching for a Dog 100
Dream # 37—The Pattern 102
Dream # 38—A Bleeding Foot 103
Dream # 39—Trip to Penn State 105
Dream # 40—Another Hug and Kiss 107
Dream # 41—Reality and the Subconscious 108
Dream # 42—The Perfect Son 109
Dream # 43—Keys to the Doorway to Heaven 111
Dream # 44—Travel Adventure 113
Dream # 45—Big Trout 116
Dream # 46—Short Visit 118
Dream # 47—Doing Good 119
Dream # 48—The Party 121

Dream # 49—Treasures in Heaven 123
Dream # 50—A Walk in Heaven 125
Dream # 51—The Beauty of God's Creation 127
Dream # 52—The Deck 129
Dream # 53—Checking on Me 131
Dream # 54—Maryland Crabs 132
Dream # 55—Fire 134
Dream # 56—Anger 136
Dream # 57—The Sickly Duck 138
Dream # 58—Consoling Carol Lee—I 140
Dream # 59—Consoling Carol Lee—II 142
Dream # 60—Carol Lee's "Passing On" 143
Dream # 61—Being Saved 145
Dream # 62—Getting Home in the Dark 148
Dream # 63—Getting Back to Carol Lee 150
Dream # 64—Sparks 153
Dream # 65—The Lost Scout Patrol 155
Dream # 66—Worship Service at St. John's Lutheran Church 158
Carol Lee: Postscript 161

In memory of my beloved wife

Carol Lee Armstrong Helton Sekula

Dreams

Introduction

In order to provide a background for this book, the following is a brief synopsis of Carol Lee's life and mine. A more complete background will be available when I finish a parallel book entitled *Carol Lee and Ed, A Beautiful Life*. My bio can also be found in "Who's Who in America" and "Who's Who in the World."

Carol Lee was born in 1940 in the little town of Mount Hope, West Virginia. I was born in 1937 in the little town of Brandonville, Pennsylvania.

Carol is part Cherokee Native American and part Scotch-Irish. The predominant occupation in the area is bituminous (soft) coal. The geography is mountainous. Her grandfather, who adopted her, worked on the railroads that carried the coal. The train, on which her grandfather rode the caboose, passed Carol Lee's house every day. She would run out to greet him. In high school, she was in the marching band. She played the alto saxophone and went on to win awards at regional competitions. After graduating from high school in West Virginia, she moved to Perryville, Maryland, to be with the mother and sister (now legally her sister and niece). She began working at the PX on Aberdeen Proving Ground, Maryland. It was there that she met me. We were married on July 13, 1963, at the post chapel. Our reception was held at the Officers Club.

My father was first-generation Polish; my grandparents immigrated to this country through Ellis Island. My father, Edward Sr., was

EDWARD J. SEKULA, JR.

born in Shenandoah, Pennsylvania. My grandfather worked in the anthracite (hard) coal mines in the area. He bought a large parcel of land in Brandonville on which he built the Sekula homestead. It was in Brandonville where he met and married my mother, Dorothy Fritz. My mother's ancestors date back to Conrad Foose born in 1795 in Sheppton, a small mining town just north of Brandonville. The Fritz family ancestors date back to the mid-1800s, when David Fritz and his family moved into the valley. Brandonville is located near the headwaters of the Catawissa Creek just south of Hazelton. It is surrounded by mountains and is in the "heart" of the anthracite area almost midway between Scranton and Harrisburg. When my father who was Roman Catholic and my mother who was Lutheran, married, they became related to almost everyone in the town of Brandonville and the valley. After graduating from high school, my father became an anthracite coal miner. Unfortunately, I never met my grandfather Sekula. He died of anthracosilicosis (miner's asthma) before I was born.

After graduating from Mahanoy Township High School, I began working in a shoe factory in Reading (fifty miles away) as a shoe cutter. After two years and becoming a skilled shoe cutter, I decided to go to the local branch campus of the Pennsylvania State University, graduating in 1961 with a BS in business administration. Having completed ROTC at Penn State, I was also commissioned a second lieutenant in the United States Army and sent to finance school at Fort Benjamin Harrison, Indiana. Just before graduating from finance school, the Berlin crisis broke out; and having graduated second in my class, instead of going to Germany like most of my classmates, I was assigned deputy finance officer of Aberdeen Proving Ground, Maryland. It was there that I met and married Carol Lee.

During my last year in college, I was awarded an internship with Peat, Marwick, Mitchell & Company in New York City. This three-month internship served as one half of my final grade. In September of 1963, I became an employee of Peat, Marwick. Carol Lee and I rented an apartment in Brooklyn where my cousin Clifford (Buddy) Kehley and his wife and children lived. In September of 1966, our only child, David, was born.

After five years in the apartment, we moved to an apartment in a new home in Staten Island, near two of my other Kehley cousins. After four years, we bought a home in Netcong, New Jersey, where Carol Lee lived the rest of her life, and I am still living.

Upon my retirement in September of 2002 at the age of sixty-five, Carol Lee contracted multiple myeloma, a terminal cancer. Obviously, our dreams to tour the United States and Europe could not be fulfilled. After forcing the cancer to recede using the drug thalidomide, Carol Lee had a stem cell transplant at Dartmouth Medical Center in New Hampshire. Our son, David, works in the cancer research laboratory at Dartmouth College and helped to arrange for his mother's transplant. The transplant consisted of harvesting Carol Lee's stem cells, freezing them, giving her a massive dose of chemotherapy, thawing the harvested stem cells, and transplanting them back into her body. The procedure could extend Carol Lee's life for up to seven years. It succeeded in extending it almost six years.

Carol Lee passed on January 27, 2008.

This book, which is dedicated to her memory, is about the dreams or, as I call them, the visits by Carol Lee from heaven.

Dream Interpretation

(http://en.wikipedia.org/wiki/Dream_interpretation)

In researching dream interpretation, I came across Wikipedia, the free encyclopedia's listing of dream interpretations. I have summarized some of the content below, but I have also added my own ideas. You may wish to read the entire content of the Web site before reading this chapter.

Basically, dream interpretation is the process of assigning meaning to dream. In ancient times, dreams were considered a supernatural communication or a method of divine intervention. The message in the dream could only be unraveled by those with special powers. Probably the greatest known person possessing these special powers of dream interpretation was Joseph. The biblical account of Joseph's interpretation of the Pharaoh's dreams led to a turning point in human history and the growth of the Judeo-Christian religions. The biblical account of Daniel indicates that he also could interpret dreams sent from God. The Bible also describes many incidences of dream. I will cover them in more detail later.

In modern times, schools of psychology have proposed theories about dream interpretation or the meaning of dreams.

Dream interpretation became a part of psychoanalysis in the late nineteenth century. Dreams were analyzed to reveal their latent meaning.

EDWARD J. SEKULA, JR.

One of the first major works on the subject was Sigmund Freud's *The Interpretation of Dreams*.

SIGMUND FREUD

Freud argued that the foundation of all dream content was wish fulfillment—that the instigation of a dream is always to be found in the day preceding the dream. On this point, I totally disagree with Freud. Very few of my dreams relate to the previous day, and I have had many, many dreams of which I have had almost total recall. I also disagree with Freud that one must be a psychologist in order to interpret dreams.

Freud also viewed dreams as compromises, which ensure that sleep is not interrupted; they succeed in representing wishes fulfilled that might otherwise disturb and waken the dreamer. Again I disagree with Freud. I almost always awaken as the result of the conclusion of a nightmare. All of my dreams of Carol Lee included in this book are the result of my awakening immediately after the dream, getting up, and recording the dream.

My fear was that if I didn't record the dream immediately, I might forget some of the details.

Freud came up with a list of distorting operations that he claimed were applied to repressed wishes in forming the dreams as recollected:

- Condensation—one dream object stands for several associations and ideas.
- Displacement—a dream object's emotional significance is separated from its real object or content and attached to an entirely different one.
- Representation—a thought is translated to visual images.
- Symbolism—a symbol replaces an action, person, or idea.

He also added secondary elaboration—the outcome of the dreamer's natural tendency to make some sort of sense or story out of the various elements of the dream. He also contended that not only was it futile but actually misleading to attempt to explain one part of the manifest content with reference to another part as if the dream somehow constituted some unified or coherent conception. Again I disagree with Freud. After reading my dreams, you be the judge.

CARL JUNG

Jung believed Freud's notion of dreams as representations of unfulfilled wishes to be simplistic and naïve. Jung believed that the scope of dream interpretation was larger, reflecting the richness and complexity of the entire unconscious. Dream symbols or figures represented an unconscious attitude perceived by the dreamer to be external personages. The people I encounter in my dreams of Carol Lee are both real, semireal or people I have never met. They are known to me but I cannot recognize their faces. In real life, I can remember faces, but have difficulty remembering the names and, in some cases, where I met them or why I know them. Jung cautioned against blindly ascribing meaning to dreams without a clear understanding of the client's personal situation. I would contend that the psychiatrist can only delve into his or her client's personality, but never know it as well as the client. Therefore, the client (dreamer) is actually more able to interpret their own dreams. Obviously, this is not true with all people. People seeing a psychiatrist have special needs. However, I would hope that many people are blessed with the ability to interpret their own dreams.

CALVIN HALL

Hall developed a theory of dreams in which dreaming is considered to be a cognitive process. A dream was simply a thought or sequence of thoughts that occur during sleep.
Dream images are visual representations of personal conceptions.

Ann Faraday

Faraday helped bring dream interpretation to the mainstream by publishing a book on do-it-yourself dream interpretation and forming groups to share and analyze dreams. She focused on the application of dreams to situations occurring in one's life. While I have not read Ann's book, I agree with relating them to situations or events in one's life.

Faraday noted that "one finding has emerged pretty firmly from modern research that the majority of dreams seem in some way to reflect things that have preoccupied our minds during the previous day or two." With my dreams of Carol Lee, I cannot agree that a majority of my dreams reflected things that have preoccupied my mind during the previous day or two. However, one might argue that Carol Lee still occupies my mind daily, and in my morning prayer each day, I thank God for the forty-four wonderful years we had together.

Dreams on the Web

Dream-sharing online and dream blogs have become popular. They allow people to post keywords or an entire dream and receive an analysis. I have never used any of these because, as I stated above, I believe I am more capable of interpreting my dreams than most anyone else.

Dreams Lists

There are also Dream Lists to which you can subscribe. I have included one in the next chapter for your information and perusal.

Like many theories, those on dream interpretation are still mostly theories. Dreams in the Bible can be considered interventions by God in human history and development. Such a theory is as valid as those listed above. We may never know for certain. If we trust in God, have faith, and love him with all our heart, mind, body, and soul, we can also accept that he may be talking to us through our dreams.

Dream List

http://lists.godspeak.cc/mailman/listinfo/dreams

There are several areas you can go for dream interpretations. One such area is the Dreams List where you can post your dream. There is no guarantee that anyone will respond to your dream, but there is always the chance that someone will.

There is a restriction on dreams that may be posted, e.g., nightmares, dreams with explicit, sexual content, those that appear to be hedonistic or dreams that appear to contradict the Bible. Their web page is http://www.godspeak.net/prophetic/ps_index.html.

Dreams posted must be biblical. Any dreams or visions that contradict the Bible are assumed to be in error.

Discussions that question the basics of the Christian faith are not permitted.

These fundamentals include the following:

> God exists as an intelligent and self-aware Being.
> God created man to be in fellowship with Him but man sinned and this separated us from that fellowship with Him.
> Jesus Christ is God incarnate, Who became human, lived among us and taught us and then died for our sins.

> Jesus Christ then rose from the dead, forever conquering sin and death.
> He ascended into heaven and will return to earth to reign forever.
> In the mean time Jesus Christ sent the Holy Spirit to indwell believers and to transform us into the image of Christ.
> The same indwelling Holy Spirit also imparts spiritual gifts into those who have accepted Jesus as their Lord.
> One of these gifts is the gift of prophecy—or God speaking through man which is still active in the Church today.

I have not posted any of my dreams on this list since I prefer to make my own interpretations. However, you may wish to do so.

Dreams In The Bible

There are many instances of dreams in the Bible. I have commented on this previously.

Most dreams in the Bible represent a communication between God and man or one of God's angels and man. The entire Qur'an (Koran) of Islam is a communication between Muhammad and the angel Gabriel. Gabriel, in Islam, is often identified with the Holy Spirit of revelations, the means by which God communicates to men.

One of the most important interpreters of the dreams in the Bible was Joseph, the eleventh son of Jacob. He had the ability to not only remember and interpret his own dream, but also to interpret the dreams of others.

Had Joseph not been sold into slavery in Egypt by his brothers, we might not have the growth of the nation of Israel, the Jewish religion, or the Christian religion. If you are not familiar with the Bible story of Joseph, please read Genesis 37:12 to 47:31. The Qur'an also devotes an entire surah (book or chapter) to Joseph (Yusuf), Surah 12:1-111. If you wish to read it, a very good English translation is The Qur'an translated by Abdullah Yusuf Ali, published by Tahrike Tarsile Qur'an Inc., Elmhurst, New York, 11373-0115.

I am not going to enumerate all the dreams or visions in the Bible, but only list a few examples such as those in the story of Joseph. If you with to discover all the dreams and visions in the Bible, you need to read the entire Bible, both Old and New Testaments.

EDWARD J. SEKULA, JR.

Old Testament

Judges 6:11-14:
(Fulfillment of a prophet's dream)

    Then the Lord's angel came to the village of Ophrah and sat under the oak tree that belonged to Joash, a man of the clan of Abiezer. His son Gideon was threshing some wheat secretly in a winepress, so that the Midianites would not see him. The Lord's angel appeared to him and said, "The Lord is with you, brave and mighty man." Then the Lord ordered him, "Go with all your strength and rescue Israel from the Midianites. I myself am sending you."

Judges 7:13-15
(Gideon and victory over the Midianites; the Lord directed Gideon to go to the Midian camp with his servant Purah.)

    When Gideon arrived, he heard a man telling a friend about a dream. He was saying, "I dreamed that a loaf of barley bread rolled into our camp and hit a tent. The tent collapsed and lay flat on the ground." His friend replied, "It is the sword of the Israelite, Gideon son of Joash. It can mean anything else. God has given him victory over Midian and our whole army." When Gideon heard about the man's dream and what it meant, he fell to his knee and worshiped the Lord.

1 Kings 3:4-14
(God's gift to King Solomon)

    On one occasion, he (Solomon) went to Gibeon to offer sacrifices because that was where the most famous altar was. He had offered hundreds of burnt offerings there in the past. That night the Lord appeared to him in a dream and ask him, "What would you like me to give you?" Solomon answered, "You always showed great love for my father, David, your servant, and he was good, loyal, and honest in his relations with you. And you have continued to show him your great and constant love by giving him a son, who today rules in his place. O

Lord God, you have let me succeed my father as king, even though I am very young and don't know how to rule. Here I am among the people you have chosen to be your own people with justice and to know the difference between good and evil. Otherwise, how would I ever be able to rule this great people of yours." The Lord was pleased that Solomon had asked for this, and so he said to him, "Because you have asked for the wisdom to rule justly, instead of long life for yourself or riches or the death of your enemies, I will do what you have asked. I will give you more wisdom and understanding than anyone has ever had before or will ever have again. I will also give you what you have not asked for: all your life, you will have wealth and honor, more than that of any other king. And if you obey me and keep my laws and commands, as your father David did, I will give you long life." Solomon woke up and realized that God had spoken to him in a dream."

Job 33:14-17
(Biblical definition of a dream)

    Although God speaks again and again, no one pays attention to what he says. At night when people are asleep, God speaks in dreams and visions. He makes them listen to what he says, and they are frightened at his warnings. God speaks to make them stop their sinning and to save them from becoming proud.

Ecclesiastes 5:1-7
(Bad dreams)

    Be careful about going to the temple. It is better to go there to learn than to offer sacrifices like foolish people who don't know right from wrong. Think before you speak, and don't make any rash promises to God. He is in heaven and you are on earth . . . So don't say any more than you have to. The more you worry, the more likely you are to have bad dream, and the more you talk, the more likely you are to say something foolish. So when you make a promise to God, keep it as quickly as possible. He has no use for a fool. Do what you promise to do. Better not to promise at all than to make a promise and not keep it. Don't let your own words lead you to sin, so that you have to tell God's priest that you didn't mean it. Why make God angry with you? Why let him destroy what you have worked for? No matter how much you dream, how much useless work you do, or how much you talk, you must still stand in awe of God.

Isaiah 29:1-2, 6-8
(Dreams of eating or drinking)

God's altar, Jerusalem itself, is doomed! The city where David camped is doomed! Let another year or two come and go, with feasts and festivals, and then God will bring disaster on the city that is called "God's altar." Suddenly and unexpectedly, the Lord Almighty will rescue with violent thunderstorms and earthquakes. He will send windstorms and raging fire; then all the armies of the nations attacking the city of God's altar, all their weapons and equipment—everything—will vanish like a dream, like something imagined in the night. All the nations that assemble to attack Jerusalem will be like a starving person who dreams he is eating and wakes up hungry, or like someone dying of thirst who dreams he is drinking and wakes up with a dry throat.

Joel 2:28-29
(The Day of the Lord)

Afterward I will pour out my Spirit on everyone: your sons and your daughters will proclaim my message; your old people will have dreams, and your young people will see visions. At that time I will pour out my Spirit even on servants, both men and women.

Daniel 4:18
(Interprets King Nebuchadnezzar)

"This is the dream I had," said King Nebuchadnezzar. "Now, Belteshazzar, tell me what it means. None of my royal advisers could tell me, but you can, because the spirit of the holy gods is in you." At this, Daniel, who is also called Beltesshazzar, was so alarmed that he could not say anything. The king said to him, "Belteshazzar, don't let the dream and its message alarm you." Belteshazzar replied, "Your Majesty, I wish that the dream and its explanation applied to your enemies and not to you. The tree, so tall that it reached the sky, could be seen by everyone in the world. Its leaves were beautiful, and it had enough fruit on it to feed the whole world. Wild animals rested under it, and birds made their nests in its branches. Your Majesty, you are the tree, tall and strong. You have grown so great that you reach the sky, and your powers extends over the whole world. While you Majesty was watching, an angel came down from heaven and said, 'Cut the tree down and destroy it, but leave the stump in the ground. Wrap a band of iron and bronze around it, and leave it there in the field with thee grass. Let the dew fall on this man, and let him live there with the animals for seven years.'

"This then is what it means, your Majesty, and this is what the Supreme God has declared will happen to you. You will be driven away from human society and will live with wild animals. For seven years you will eat grass like an ox and sheep in the open air, where the dew will fall on you. Then you will admit that the Supreme God controls all human kingdoms and that he can give them to anyone he chooses. The angel ordered the stump to left in the ground. This means that you will become king again when you acknowledge that God rules all the world. So then your Majesty, follow my advice. Stop sinning, do what is right, and be merciful to the poor. Then you will continue to be prosperous."

New Testament

Luke 1:26-33
(The Announcement of the Birth of Jesus)

In the sixth month of Elizabeth's (a cousin of Mary) pregnancy (with John the Baptist) God sent the angel Gabriel to a town in Galilee named Nazareth. He had a message for a young woman promised in marriage to a man named Joseph, who was a descendent of King David. Her name was Mary. The angel came to her and said, "Peace be with you! The Lord is with you and has greatly blessed you." Mary was deeply troubled by the angel's message, and she wondered what his words meant. The angel said to her, "Don't be afraid, Mary; God has been gracious to you. You will become pregnant and give birth to a son, and you will name him Jesus. He will be great and will be called the Son of the Most High God." (If you wish to read further, Mary's Song of Praise follows).

Matthew 1:18-24
(The Birth of Jesus)

This is how the birth of Jesus Christ took place. His mother Mary was engaged to Joseph, but before they were married, she found out she was going to have a baby by the Holy Spirit. Joseph was a man who always did what was right, but he did not want to disgrace Mary publicly; so he made plans to break the engagement privately. While he was thinking about this, an angel of the Lord appeared to him in a dream and said, "Joseph, descendant of David, do not be afraid to take Mary as your wife. For it is by the Holy Spirit that she has conceived. She will have a son, and you will name him Jesus—because he will save his people form their sins." Now all this happened in order to make come true what the Lord had said through the prophet. "A virgin will become pregnant and have a son, and he will be called Immanuel [which means "God is with us"]." So when Joseph woke up, he married Mary as the angel of the Lord had told him to. But he had no sexual relations with her before she gave birth to her son. And Joseph named him "Jesus."

Matthew 2:8-15
(Shepherds in the Fields)

There were some shepherds in that part of the country who were spending the night in the fields, taking care of their flocks. An angel of the Lord appeared to them, and the glory of the Lord shone over them. They were terribly afraid, but the angel of the Lord said to them, "Don't be afraid! I am here with good news for you, which will bring great joy to all the people. This very day in David's town your Savior was born—Christ the Lord! And this is what will prove it to you: you will find the baby wrapped in cloths and lying in a manger." Suddenly a great army of heaven's angels appeared with the angel, singing praises to God: "Glory to God in the highest heaven, and peace on earth to those with whom he is pleased."

Matthew 2:13-15
(Escape to Egypt)

After they had left, an angel of the Lord appeared in a dream to Joseph and said, "Herod will be looking for the child in order to kill him. So get up, take the child and his mother and escape to Egypt, and stay there until I tell you to leave." Joseph got up, took the child and his mother, and left during the night for Egypt, where he stayed until Herod died. This was done to make come true what the Lord had said through the prophet, "I called my Son out of Egypt."

Matthew 2:19-21
(Return to Israel)

"After Herod died, an angel of the Lord appeared in a dream to Joseph in Egypt and said, 'Get up, take the child and his mother, and go back to the land of Israel, because those who tried to kill the child are dead.' So Joseph got up, took the child and his mother and went back to Israel."

Matthew 27:19
(Pilate's wife's dream)

While Pilate was sitting in the judgment hall, his wife sent a message to him: "Have nothing to do with that innocent man, because in a dream I suffered much on account of him." (Lutheran theology: "On account of Christ, our sins are forgiven").

EDWARD J. SEKULA, JR.

Acts 2:16-21
(Peter's Message)

Instead (of being drunk as the people supposed), this is what the prophet Joel spoke about:

> "This is what I will do in the last days," God says:
> "I will pour out my Spirit to everyone.
> Your sons and daughters will proclaim my message;
> Your young me will see visions,
> And your old men will have dreams.
>
> Yes even on my servants, both men and women,
> I will pour out my Spirit in those days,
> And they will proclaim my message.
> I will perform miracles in the sky above and wonders on the earth below.
> There will be blood, fire and thick smoke; the sun will be darkened, and the moon will turn red as blood, before the great and glorious Day of the Lord comes.
>
> And then, whoever calls out to the Lord for help will be saved."

My Dreams

I have been blessed with a unique ability. Not only do I dream in vivid Technicolor, but I have almost total recall of my dreams.

When I was six years old, I began having a repeating nightmare. I was wrestling with Satan, and he "zapped" me with an energy force that totally paralyzed my body. The only thing I could move was my eyes, but since my head was paralyzed in place, my vision was extremely limited. Depending on which way I was sleeping, I could only look in that direction. At first, the vision appeared to be in the exact detail as if I were awake. It was not until my midteens that I was able to break this recurring nightmare. My parents and I were living in a rented home in Swank's Grove. My bedroom was on the second floor under the eaves that formed a V across my bed. On one side of the bed was my small roller top desk. Being very neat, everything on the desk had a place, and everything was always in its place. This final nightmare, I was paralyzed in a position where all I could see was the inside of my roller desk. Whether it was my conscious entering my subconscious, I am not sure, but I observed one item that was out of place in my nightmare. I immediately awoke and never had that nightmare again.

A second dream where my conscious seemed to enter my subconscious (or dream) was when I was a freshman at Penn State. Going to the Pottsville Campus for my first two years allowed me to commute from my home in Brandonville. I spent almost an hour trying to solve a complex algebra equation and finally gave up and went to bed. In the middle of the night, again whether it was my subconscious (dream) or conscious entering my subconscious, I do not know. While dreaming, I was able to solve the equation. I woke and immediately wrote down the solution.

The first dream I recorded was after we had moved to New Jersey. It was probably in the late seventies because David was still going to Netcong Elementary School. We had just purchased an IBM Selectric typewriter at a school auction. It was my first major dream about Carol Lee:

Carol Lee and I were attending worship service at St. John's Lutheran Church in Brandonville. The church was a two-story old-style wooden building. The outside was painted white. Upon entering, we ascended the wide staircase leading to the second floor. The worship area consisted of an altar at the back of the building with a picture of Jesus in a white gown with outstretched arms hanging over the altar. The pews were the standard wooden pews on each side of the worship area separated by an aisle running from the top of the stairs to the altar. Carol Lee always liked to sit in one of the front pews, so we went up front and sat down. As soon as the worship service started, some yelled "fire." There was panic. The worshipers in the front of the building ran for the stairs. Everyone else was trying to push their way toward the stairs. In the ensuing panic, Carol Lee and I got separated. The crowd pushed me to the steps and outside. I suddenly realized I had one of Carol Lee's shoes in my hand, but I could not see Carol Lee. I looked through the crowd and suddenly realized that she wasn't there. She was back in the flaming building. I had lost her. The flame engulfing the two-story wooden building reached high into the sky. As I looked upward, I saw God holding in his hands the Book of Life. He looked at me and said, "Don't worry. Her name is written in the Book of Life." He then opened the book and showed me her name on a page in the book. I woke up.

I immediately went downstairs and typed the dream on our newly acquired typewriter. It was the first dream I ever recorded.

My interpretation of the dream was that I never had to worry about Carol Lee. She was destined to be in the "hands of God," to be in his presence, to be in heaven. I, on the hand, had no direct assurance from God except for my faith. So I strive to strengthen my faith every day so that someday in the future, I can be reunited with my beloved Carol Lee, and together we can praise God and sing to his Glory throughout all eternity.

Thirty years later, on January 27, 2008, after battling to stay alive for over seven and a half hours, I said to Carol Lee, "It's OK, let go, go to God," and she immediately flatlined. I knew she was in God's hands. Her name was written in the "Book of Life."

On February 1, 2008, Carol Lee's funeral service was held at St. John's Lutheran Church in Brandonville—the very same church in the dream. She was buried in the cemetery adjacent to the church as our great-grandparents, grandparents, mother, and father; and someday I will be laid to rest beside her.

Luke 10:20
Jesus said, "Be glad because your names are written."

In Memory Of
Carol Lee Armstrong Helton Sekula

May 1, 1940—January 27, 2008

Carol Lee was the love of my life. Only the light of God shines brighter in my heart. She was the most beautiful soul I have ever met. She was my beautiful Southern belle. I was proud of her part Cherokee Native American ancestry. For over forty-four years, God blessed us with one of the most beautiful marriages I have ever known. Like my parents before, our love was an unspoken love. The word did not have to be spoken. It was shared. It was lived. We grew so close that we often knew what the other was about to say. Often we began saying the exact same words and would stop and just look at each other and smile or laugh.

Her love for our son, David, and his family was as great as her love for me. Her love for her sister Liz and her family was as deep as her love for me. When asked to speak at Liz and Ken's fiftieth anniversary party, I said I knew no two sisters as close as those two.

Carol Lee was a beautiful soul who touched everyone she came into contact with. She never had an unkind word for anyone. I shall miss her for the rest of my life. I shall love her for the rest of my life. It is not in death that we shall part, for our love shall exist through all eternity. I know that she is now with God and that someday I will again join her. Her name is written in the "Book of Life." Many years ago, God revealed this to me in a dream.

The dream is now complete!

For almost six years, from the date of my retirement party in 2002, she battled with multiple myeloma cancer. She fought the battle with dignity and without complaint. She was a fighter. In her final week, she paid me the highest compliment that I had ever received in my life. She called me her "rock," but in fact, she had always been my "rock."

In her final hour, when the hospital harpist was playing "Amazing Grace" just outside the door to her room, I knew the angels were calling her home. In her final moments, as she was struggling to keep breathing, I looked at my beautiful Carol Lee and said to her, "Let it go, it's OK, go to God," and instantaneously she "flatlined." I knew God had instantaneously answered my prayer, and she is now in his hands.

Carol Lee, I love you, and I shall love you the rest of my life and throughout all eternity. You shall be my inspiration for the rest of my life. I shall never forget you, my beautiful love.

Your Ed forever!

My First Dream Of Carol Lee From Heaven

January 30, 2008—4:10 AM

Gateway to Heaven

The dream started like one of our usual travel log dreams but different in type and ending. We were traveling on a motorbike over a mountain trail. (The trail resembled that of the one on top of the mountain at Massanutten but was a bike trail.) Each of us had a backpack strapped to our backs. (We were never on a mountain bike—John had one, and Carol Lee never wore a backpack.) As we traveled over the mountain trail with its beautiful scenery, we came upon a rest station (like our trips to New Hampshire). We took off our backpacks and took things out of them (presumably food, just like our stops at the Connecticut rest area). We then got back on our motorbike with me driving and her with her arms around me. After traveling a while, we came to the end of the bike trail. It was a wooden platform with a wooden railing on both sides and a wooden gate leading to walking-only path (the entrance to heaven). We got off the bike, and Carol Lee took off her backpack. When I went to take off mine, I realized it wasn't there. I must have lost it on the trail or left it back at the last rest station. (Carol Lee leaving her pocketbook behind and us hoping that it would still be there when we went back for it—we always got it back.) She told me to go back and look for it. She would wait there for me. As I got back on the bike, I realized the bike had a flat tire, but I got on it and, with great difficulty, started backtracking. (She had gone on before me, and my road back would be a difficult one.) I got back to the rest station, and there were about six people there. I couldn't find it. So I called out, "Has anyone seen an orange backpack?" (Orange is Tyler's favorite color.) A stranger with two young boys (about Cub Scout age) answered. "Yes! It is in the washing machine, it was dirty so I took the items out of it and put it in the machine." (My new life will be different; it will be clean and strangers will help me.)

While waiting for the backpack to be washed, one of the strangers, two young boys, offered me what looked like a bottle of soda to drink. (This was the scout at the jamboree who offered me a drink of his water when it looked like I wasn't going to make it up the last hill I had to climb.) When I started to take a drink, I realized it wasn't soda. I had to shake it to get it to the top of the bottle. It looked like uncooked but moist brownie mix. (Our neighbors Nancy and Dan had visited us just before I went to bed, and she had brought over brownies for us to eat.) As I began taking the mix into my mouth, it came out like string, and the stranger cautioned me, "It is very rich, don't eat too much of it." (Carol Lee was telling me that the rest of my life would be "very rich" but cautioned me to go slow and not take too much. She was also telling me that she was waiting for me.)

I woke up vividly remembering the entire dream, which was in vivid color.

Dream # 2

A Picture of Heaven

February 6, 2008—1:30 PM

I was downstairs in our home, either doing one of my chores or watching TV as I was accustomed to doing. (The beginning is a bit fussy, so I'm not quite sure which it was.)

I heard Carol Lee calling me. As usual, I was slow to respond. Finally, I dashed upstairs, and there was Carol Lee sitting at our dining room table. She was all dressed up, wearing her glasses and a hat. She was waiting for me to take her somewhere. She had a frown or a forlorn look on her face because she had to wait for me. (It was a look I had seen many times when she was here on earth with me.) There was one major difference to the scene:

We have a chandelier hanging from the ceiling over the table. The table is usually cluttered with documents, fruit basket, boxes, etc. The table in the dream was completely empty. Instead of the chandelier hanging from the ceiling, the lighting fixture was sitting in the middle of the table, almost covering it. It looked like a glass castle with spirals pointing toward the ceiling. Each spiral was emanating either purple (Carol Lee's favorite color) or green. (My favorite color—for me, green is the color of life.)

In the spring, I sit in my "prayer chair" in our backyard and watch the grass and plants turn green; I watch the trees bud and turn into green leaves. In the summer, the grass is a luscious green, and the leaves on the trees are a beautiful green. I thank God for his beautiful creation: the universe; our planet earth with its beautiful plants, trees, and animals; and especially humankind—his select children to whom he has sent the prophets and his Son Jesus so that we might know him and his kingdom and that Jesus is the "Way" for us to enter the kingdom.) The beautiful light on the table was like none I had ever seen before. Surely, this dream is from Carol Lee in heaven. She is there and is waiting for me to come running so that we can begin our journey through eternity.

Dream # 3

"Pooky"

This was one of the shortest dreams of Carol visiting me.

She was standing in the doorway dressed in a beautiful black-and-white polka-dot dress and wearing a beautiful black-and-white polka-dot hat with a very wide brim.

(Last week, David, Gina, and I had walked through Walmart, and the memory of Carol's and my last shopping trip came to mind, and I lost it; tears came streaming down my cheek. We had been looking for a new winter hat to keep her head warm. She wanted a black one, but the kind they had didn't come in black. The closest she could find was a specked black and white—almost polka-dot.)

Standing beside Carol in the doorway is our dog, Buttons, or "Pooky" as we affectionately called her.

(I had a picture of Buttons on Carol's dresser, and David showed it to Gina, explaining to her that we used to affectionately call Buttons "Pooky.")

I waved good-bye to Carol and Buttons and was off on one of my adventures. Oddly, I didn't recall the details of that adventure.

Dream # 4

WALKING IN THE PRESENCE OF GOD

March 8, 2008—5:00 AM

Carol Lee and I were at a conference or other dinner event. We were leaving the dining room and walking down a very long hallway (similar to our last Rotary conference in the Catskills or the one down at Hershey). We were among the first out of the room. (This was usual for us; we wanted to beat the crowds.) There were only a few people walking with us. As we were walking, someone called out my name, and I turned. He said, "Come over here, there are some friends of yours from college." So I left Carol Lee standing beside a table in the hallway. The other people leaving were going around the table and her. I went back to see who was calling me and who these friends might be. As usual, the faces were familiar, but I couldn't recall their names. After greeting them, I turned back to Carol Lee and began walking toward her. I saw that Bob Jacques's wife (I sat across the table from her at the Sunapee District of the Daniel Webster Council BSA annual dinner in New Hampshire two nights before) was standing at the table with her. When they saw me coming toward them, they started walking down the hallway knowing I would catch up to them. All of a sudden, the hallway was filled with people. Everyone was now coming out of the dining room. I no longer could see Carol Lee ahead of me. I looked all around the crowd but no Carol Lee. I began to panic. Where was she? I had lost her.

EDWARD J. SEKULA, JR.

This is a type of dream I often have. I would get separated from the group I was with and either could not catch up or find them. Often I didn't know where I was or how to get back to my room or hotel. I would get so frantic in my dream that I would wake up, but this time I didn't. I never before had a dream like this involving Carol Lee.

In my dream, all of a sudden there was Carol Lee waiting for me. I was so happy to find her. We continued to walk down the hallway together, and I woke up.

For now, I have lost the physical presence of Carol Lee. I will find her again in heaven, and we will "walk on" together in the presence of God through all eternity.

*　　*　　*

An event similar to the dream had actually occurred at our Rotary Hershey conference.

We were leaving the conference. I was taking the suitcases out to the van. Carol Lee was back, closing up our room and making sure we had gotten everything out of the room—our usual procedure. She would then lock the room and come out to the van. I would usually go back toward the room to meet her and help her out. She wasn't in the hallway. I couldn't see her. I went back to our room, but she had already left it and locked it. I didn't know where she could be. I had lost her. I began to panic. Carol Lee had a poor sense of direction, and often when we came out of a room or store, she would turn in the wrong direction. So I headed down the hallway in the opposite direction to the next exit. There were exits at the end of each hallway that formed a very long circle. I kept going to the next and the next all the way around the building, getting more frantic as I went. What could have happened to her? Where was she? I had lost her and couldn't find her. After circling the building, I got back to our exit, and there she was—standing and waiting for me. How happy I was to see (find) her. Together, we walked out to the van and drove home.

Dream # 5

"Her Rock"

May 18, 2008—6:00 AM

Carol Lee and I were talking. Carol was scolding me for not doing something the way she wanted it done. I countered by saying I tried to do it the best I could.

(This actually occurred several times especially in her last year. I often fell short of her expectations. I felt guilty then and now because I couldn't do more for her or do things exactly the way Carol Lee wanted me to do them. As her cancer had progressed in 2007, it became more and more difficult for her to do normal things. The more difficult it became, the harder I tried to please her, but the more I fell short. It was the cancer, not my efforts.)

The dream progressed, and a friend (I couldn't identify her), well dressed and very professional looking, came to my aid. She told Carol Lee she was expecting too much from me. That I was trying to please her even though I may have fallen short of her expectations.

In 2007, I had purchased for her a new mattress, a scooter, clothes (size 14), toilet riser, shower head, ice spikes for her cane, etc.

In a pamphlet, *Going On . . . A Pathway Through Sorrow*, by Jane Woods Shoemaker (sent to me by USAA), feeling guilty is a common effect of losing a spouse. Often they are intense with regrets of wishing that we had been more loving and understanding, less demanding, given her more attention (done more for her). While I believe I tried my best and had done all that I could do, I still know I could have done more.

In the dream, I believe Carol Lee was telling me not to feel guilty. She understands that I am trying my best. That was why in the last days she called me her "rock."

Dream # 6

LIFE IN HEAVEN IS EASY AND FUN

May 19, 2008—5:00 AM

It was another adventure dream. I was off walking through the woods on the top of a mountain with the Kehley boys: Buddy, Sonny, Billy, Tommy, and Bobby. Suddenly, we came to an open section of the forest and a six-foot wall of snow and ice. We climbed up to the top of it with ease and kept going. At first, it was difficult to cross, more like a glacier than snow. Then we came to an area with rocks sticking above the ice and snow, and we were able to jump from one rock to another, again with ease. It was a lot of fun. Suddenly, we reached the edge of the mountain, and it was a very steep slope to the bottom. One of the Kehleys said, "Let's go explore the caves at the bottom of the mountain." While it was extremely steep, it was an easy climb to the bottom. I got to the caves first but couldn't go inside. The melting snow and ice had caused large streams of water to flow out from inside the caves. The streams flowed into a swampy area with pools of water that were frozen. (These were similar to the pond in my backyard.) We began clearing limbs and branches for the frozen pools (which I planned to do but have not been able to do in pool in my backyard) so that we could ice skate from one pool to the next. When we were done, I realized it was a much larger pond than the one in my backyard and would be much better for skating. I wished I had not forgotten my ice skates, but I began skating with just my boots. It was easy. I was skating faster than I could have if I had my ice skates on. It was so much fun. Suddenly, I hit a patch of thin

EDWARD J. SEKULA, JR.

ice. I couldn't stop. The thin ice turned into unfrozen water, and I fell in, getting all wet. I told the boys I needed to go back to the house and get dry clothes. Immediately, I was in a warm home, and I was wearing dry clothes. I was sitting at a table. Mae and Cliff Kehley were sitting with me. I looked at Cliff and realized Cliff had passed away. I said to myself, "Oh my God, we have all passed away. We are in heaven." At that point, Carol Lee joined Cliff, Mae, and me at the table; and I woke up.

What fun and joy and happiness heaven must be.

Dream # 7

FISHING IN HEAVEN

June 7, 2008—6:00 AM

Carol Lee, David, and I were beside a small stream. Carol Lee was fishing. (She had only fished with me a dozen times or less in our forty-four years of marriage, and a week of them was on our "honeymoon" in Canada where we stayed in a small cabin without a door or windows—another story in another book.)

This was a beautiful small but fast flowing stream, and Carol Lee was fishing it by walking beside it. I told her to let her lure, which was a flashing gold spinner, drifting down the stream in front of her as she walked. I told her that if there were any fish in this stream, they would hit the flashing gold spinner, which we all could see. She was fishing the lure perfectly. David and I were walking beside her and watching the spinner. If a fish hit the spinner, we would see it hit.

Suddenly, we came to a high cliff of rocks on the opposite side of the stream. As we got closer, we could see that the rocks were not natural. They were stacked one on top of the other, going up very high like a man-made cliff. As we got closer, I recognized the inscriptions on the rocks—Aztec (Mayan). Looking upward, we now could see it was a beautiful Aztec pyramid. We could see a small hillside behind us opposite the pyramid, and I said we needed to get further back to truly appreciate the beauty of the pyramid.

EDWARD J. SEKULA, JR.

I woke up.

I had always wanted Carol Lee to learn to fish and go fishing with me, but she wasn't the outdoors type and left the fishing to me. I had also always wanted to vacation in Cancun or Kozumel and visit one or more of the Mayan/Aztec pyramids. While we didn't get to do it in real life, we did it in a dream. It was wonderful that David was with us in the dream. Maybe the three of us can actually go fishing and visit the pyramids in heaven.

One interpretation is that the three of us can be together again in heaven and appreciate its beauty.

Some time after this dream, I came across a picture of a Mayan pyramid that was almost the exact image of the one in my dream. You explain it!

Dream # 8

WATCHING OVER ME—I

July 9, 2008—4:00 AM

I'm in the orchard of the Sekula homestead (where we hold our annual Sekula family reunion over Labor Day). A storm moves in. It has heavy lightning and thunder. The clouds get very dark. I start running for the house, but it starts raining before I can get there. I get soaking wet. Inside the house, I find Carol Lee (no one else). She is getting ready to watch a movie on TV.

Instead of being in front of the TV, we are now in a movie theater. We are in the last row, but instead of sitting in the middle, Carol Lee moves to the other end of the row of seats. I motion to her to come to the middle, but she motions for me to come to her at the end of the row. So I do. (My grandson Tyler and I had gone to the movie theater the day before and sat not in the middle, but almost at the end of the row.)

As I sit beside her, I realize that I am very cold having been soaked by the rain. Carol Lee is wearing a long flowing skirt. I am wearing shorts. She wraps her skirt around my legs, and instantly, I am warm.

The movie starts. There is a Native American king and queen in a coffin with a glass top so you can see their faces and their entire bodies. They are not dressed in traditional North American clothing. Their clothing is more like Mayan or Aztec. The queen speaks, "We were unable to be married in life, but now we will be married in death."

The scene changes. The queen is back with her tribe, which is located near what is now Boston. She takes her tribe and all her wealth and begins to travel across the United States to Los Angeles where the king of his tribe is waiting to marry her.

The scene again changes to a map of the United States, showing the trail she is taking.

All the states are identified on the map. (If I were to sit down and attempt to draw a map of all the states in the United States, I could not. Not many people could.) She travels from Boston across New York, Pennsylvania, Ohio, Indiana, Illinois, Missouri, Texas, and then on to California. When she gets there, she finds that the king is dead.

I wake up.

Interpretation:

Storms in my life can be calmed by Carol Lee's memory. She is my guardian angel. If I am wet and cold, she can warm me. Death has no control over love. Even after death, two people who deeply love each other can get together (in heaven) even now while one of them is still alive. I have no doubt they will be together in heaven after both have passed on.

The trip taken by the queen across the United States is exactly opposite that taken by early Native Americans. In a presentation I do on Native Americans (North American),

I consider two paths from west to east. One is down the Pacific coast from Alaska and then east at the bottom of the Rocky Mountains (the reverse of the trip the queen had taken in my dream). The other is down the eastern slope of the Rocky Mountains from Canada to the Missouri River, then down the Missouri to its juncture with the Ohio, which then forms the Mississippi River. They then would have traveled up the Ohio to the Allegheny River and Lake Erie. From there, they would travel east to Maine (Boston in the dream). At the juncture of the Allegheny and Monongahela Rivers, another group could have separated from the main group and traveled down the Monongahela River to the southern Appalachian Mountains from West Virginia to Georgia—the Cherokee nation, Carol Lee's ancestors. However, more recent history indicates that the Cherokee may have traveled east from Texas and Oklahoma east to Georgia. They then traveled north up the Appalachian Mountains where they came in contact with the Iroquois and the Lenni Lenape. The Cherokee and Iroquois nations were considered the most civilized of all the tribes by the early settlers.

If this later route is the actual one taken by the Cherokees, then as a result of the Indian round up and relocation to Indian Territory (Oklahoma) in the west, a journey where almost half the Cherokee nation died on "The Trail of Tears," Carol Lee's ancestors would be the group of Cherokee, now known as the Eastern Cherokee tribe, who escaped the round up. Some fleeing as far north as West Virginia where Carol Lee was born.

Dream # 9

WATCHING TV TOGETHER

July 28, 2009—4:00 AM

I'm dreaming that I am sleeping on the couch with the TV on. I hear a noise. Carol Lee is coming down the steps to our recreation room. I wake up (in my dream) and see her coming down the steps. I say, "I'm glad to see you. I was getting lonely down here." She comes down and sits on the couch with me. We're on our "love seat." We both start to watch TV, but soon I fall asleep (in my dream).

I wake up.

I remember the dream. Obviously, I am alone and miss her terribly. If only she could once again come down the steps and watch TV with me.

Before Carol Lee passed on, she almost never came down to our recreation room to watch TV with me. She had great difficulty getting up and down stairs, especially getting back up them. So that she didn't have to go up and down our stairs to watch TV, I purchased and installed one in her bedroom, hooking it up to our cable network. After contracting multiple myeloma, she spent most of her days lying in bed and watching her own TV. The time we did spend together were extremely precious, especially our "road trips"—virtually every time we got into our van. Even her trips to the doctor (s) or hospital became a "road trip" for us. These truly were precious times together.

Dream # 10

SEEING CAROL LEE

August 6, 2008—10:00 PM
(Almost the same dream as Dream # 9)

I fall asleep watching TV. I'm awakened by Carol Lee coming down the steps.

I wake up.

She is not there. I'm bewildered. Then I remember, Carol Lee is no longer with me. She has passed on. I'll never be with her again in this life. When I pass on, we will once more be joined together and our sparks of life will continue together through all eternity. We will be singing praises to God along with all the angels throughout all eternity.

Dream # 11

Last Kiss

August 10, 2008—1:00 AM

I have just fallen asleep. Carol Lee is sitting in a chair looking as beautiful as ever. I'm holding her hand. I'm looking at her, and I realize she is slipping away. Her usual smile leaves her face, and we both realize she doesn't have much time left. I kiss her on the forehead, knowing that this would be the last time I will kiss her.

Suddenly, I wake up.

The last five days of Carol Lee's life were my most difficult. Her face completely changed. I almost didn't recognize her. In her final hours, I held her hand continuously. Once in a while, I could feel a little squeeze even though her eyes were closed. In addition to the monitor, you could see in her face that her life was slowly slipping away from her. When she finally let go and went into God's hands, I was still holding her hand.

I kissed her on the forehead.

Our last kiss.

Dream # 12

CRYSTAL ICE CAVE

September 10, 2008—1:00 AM

Carol Lee and I are walking in a beautiful park/garden. I have never seen anything comparable on earth. It is extremely beautiful. It is crowded like an amusement park, but the people are extremely peaceful and calm. No one is rushing about, cutting you off, or pushing you. The predominant feature of the park is a "crystal ice cave" located near the top of a hill in the center of the park. Walking paths crisscross through the garden with some of them going up to the crystal ice cave. The cave is pure white with crystal clear icicles hanging from the roof.

Suddenly, I am hungry. Almost out of nowhere, there is a table full of cakes in front of me. I begin eating the cakes, but notice Carol Lee is no longer with me. I look all around, but cannot see her. (This is similar to many of my dreams where we become separated, and I cannot find her.) Again, I have lost her. (She has "passed on"; the greatest fear in all my dreams is that I will never find her again.)

I begin walking and looking for her. She is nowhere to be found. As I am walking, I see my mother and my father (both have passed on). I ask them if they have seen Carol Lee. Dad says, "Yes, we just passed her. She was walking up the path to the 'crystal ice cave.'"

Happily, I too begin walking up the path to the crystal ice cave knowing that I soon would be with Carol Lee again.

I wake up.

The park is in "heaven." Carol Lee is in the "crystal ice palace" of heaven, and I am walking up the pathway (faith in Jesus Christ, the "gateway to heaven") to heaven to meet her once again. There we can spend eternity together in the presence of God and sing his praises throughout all eternity.

Dream # 12

CRYSTAL ICE CAVE

September 10, 2008—1:00 AM

Carol Lee and I are walking in a beautiful park/garden. I have never seen anything comparable on earth. It is extremely beautiful. It is crowded like an amusement park, but the people are extremely peaceful and calm. No one is rushing about, cutting you off, or pushing you. The predominant feature of the park is a "crystal ice cave" located near the top of a hill in the center of the park. Walking paths crisscross through the garden with some of them going up to the crystal ice cave. The cave is pure white with crystal clear icicles hanging from the roof.

Suddenly, I am hungry. Almost out of nowhere, there is a table full of cakes in front of me. I begin eating the cakes, but notice Carol Lee is no longer with me. I look all around, but cannot see her. (This is similar to many of my dreams where we become separated, and I cannot find her.) Again, I have lost her. (She has "passed on"; the greatest fear in all my dreams is that I will never find her again.)

I begin walking and looking for her. She is nowhere to be found. As I am walking, I see my mother and my father (both have passed on). I ask them if they have seen Carol Lee. Dad says, "Yes, we just passed her. She was walking up the path to the 'crystal ice cave.'"

Happily, I too begin walking up the path to the crystal ice cave knowing that I soon would be with Carol Lee again.

I wake up.

The park is in "heaven." Carol Lee is in the "crystal ice palace" of heaven, and I am walking up the pathway (faith in Jesus Christ, the "gateway to heaven") to heaven to meet her once again. There we can spend eternity together in the presence of God and sing his praises throughout all eternity.

Dream # 13

FISHING TRIP

September 14, 2008—5:30 AM

I'm fishing down a river, trolling with one fishing rod (I usually use two). I'm in a rowboat similar to the one I used to fish from with my father and mother. There are two rods in the boat, but only one of them is mine. It is a beautiful stretch of water. Ahead of me is a beautiful riffle where I'm sure I will catch a fish. I steer the boat to the top of the riffle near the far shore.

All of a sudden, I hook a very large fish. As I am battling the fish, I notice several campsites on the shore where other fishermen are preparing their breakfast (it is morning). I keep trying to reel the large fish into the boat, but cannot. The current is taking me and the fish all the way downstream through the riffle. The fish makes several jumps out of the water. I see that it is long and slender. It must be a trout, but I'm not sure. All of a sudden, the fish breaks off, and I lose it. I reel in my line and lure and find that there is a piece of the fish's skin still on the lure. It is from a very large brown trout, and I am sad that I had lost it.

The battle had taken me all the way down the riffle. I am now in a very large pool that flowed through a small town. The town is on both sides of the river. On the one side, the street is against the river bank. I am drifting very close to the bank and the street.

EDWARD J. SEKULA, JR.

I'm looking forward in the boat when suddenly out of nowhere (but apparently from the street) someone jumps into the boat behind me. I turn and see that it is Carol Lee.

Carol Lee picks up the other rod and begins fishing. We are almost out of the town when I see "white water" rapids just ahead of us. So I row the boat to shore and say that we can't go any further. We will have to go back upstream.

Carol Lee says, "Let's get out of the boat and sit on the shore for a while." We can still see the little town on both sides of the river. Carol Lee says she would like a cup of coffee. A woman and her son come and sit down beside us. I ask her if there is somewhere I can buy a cup of coffee in the town. She replies, "Just down the street."

As I am about to leave Carol Lee and go for the coffee, I wake up.

Once again in my dream, Carol Lee and I come to an impasse—the "white water."
But strangers helped us, and I must leave Carol Lee. She goes to God, and I must remain on earth for a time before I can rejoin her in heaven, in the presence of God where we can sing praises to God throughout all eternity.

Dream # 14

Losing Carol Lee—Again

October 4, 2008—4:00 AM

I'm dreaming that I'm still half awake and lying in bed. Carol Lee has already gotten up.

I don't see her, but I can hear her going down our stairs. She calls to me and tells me she is going to the store. I continue to lie in bed instead of getting up. I plan to lie there until Carol Lee gets back from the store, and then I will get up.

I hear a car in the driveway and then someone coming up the steps. I believe it is Carol Lee. They call to me, but it is not Carol Lee. It is Pat, my fishing buddy. He asks me where I am, and I tell him I am in the bedroom. He comes in and just looks at me. I can tell something bad has happened to Carol Lee. That she will never be coming home again.

I wake up.

Jeanie, Pat, and I had just spent the night before—talking, eating, and playing cards.

Both Pat and Jeanie along with Millie Miller were with me at Carol Lee's bedside when she passed on. I thank God for friends like them.

Dream # 15

A "Treatser"

October 11, 2008

I have just come home from a fishing trip. Carol Lee is standing there at the door to greet me. She tells me she has a "treatser" for me in the refrigerator.

I wake up.

Carol Lee loved to bake. On our first date, she had baked me a cherry pie, and I ate almost the whole pie. I was "hooked" on her.

Even when she was so ill that it was difficult for her to get out of bed, she would get up and bake a pie or cake for me—a "treatser."

When she was well enough to go for a ride in the van, we would go out for a "treatser."
This was usually to Cliff's for a small ice cream cone (a twist) or a root beer float. We both knew we were breaking our diets, but we treated ourselves anyway.

I still either bake a small cake or pie for myself or go out for a "treatser." I probably will until I can no longer do so.

Dream # 16

CAROL LEE CALLING

October 17. 2008—7:00 AM

I'm in a very deep sleep (usually I wake up every morning between 6:00 and 7:00 AM, but today I was in a deep sleep).

I hear Carol Lee calling my name, "Ed, Ed," and I wake up.

One of the things I miss most since Carol Lee's passing on is hearing her call my name.
Usually, I would be downstairs, and she would be in her bed. Usually, she was calling me because she needed something, or she wanted to tell me something.

Since January 27, when she passed on, I often hear her calling "Ed."

Usually, it is when I have fallen asleep downstairs while watching TV that I hear her calling me. I wake up, turn the TV off, and go upstairs to bed.

This is the first time I am already upstairs and in bed and in a very deep, deep sleep.

I do miss her calling "Ed."

Dream # 17

Working

October 20, 2008—4:00 AM

I'm at home. Carol Lee comes home from work. She looks very tired and haggard. She almost doesn't look like herself.

I tell her that if her work is causing her to be so tired, she didn't have to work. We would be OK (financially).

I ask her what section of Baltimore she was working (?????—Carol Lee never worked in Baltimore. It is a very long drive, and I didn't want her working in a bad section of the city.)

I wake up.

A similar event happened to Carol Lee and me when we were living in Brooklyn. The unemployment agency had sent her to a job on the Brooklyn docks. Even though she lost her unemployment benefit a one day's pay, when I found out that night, I wouldn't let her go back to the job.

Also, one job Carol Lee had was a long drive from Netcong. After a few months, she found a job closer to home.

The way she looked in the dream was the way she looked in her final days. Her face had changed so much you could hardly recognize her.

Dream # 18

REMEMBERING

October 21, 2008—6:00 AM

October 21, Carol Lee calls my name, "Ed," and I wake up from a very deep sleep. I remember that I had not recorded my dream on the twentieth. I got up and recorded the dream.

Last night, October 20, 2008, I had to drive to our Boy Scout headquarters in Florham Park for a meeting. On the way down and back, I remembered the many trips I made taking Carol Lee to Morristown Memorial Hospital, especially her last days.

During her last days, I would go to the hospital in the morning and come back home at night when it was dark, just like it was coming home from the Patriots' Path Council, BSA meeting.

I also remembered her last week and days in the hospital—how "tired" and "haggard" she looked. She didn't look like herself.

I also, once again, recounted the last hours of her life.

On the way to the hospital, after receiving a voice mail from both her doctor and her nurse to come the hospital as quickly as possible, I prayed to God and Jesus asking them to save her. I must have repeated the prayer a thousand or more times. My mouth got so dry that I had to repeat the prayer in my mind.

As I approached the hospital, I realized why am I asking Jesus to save her? He has already saved her by sacrificing his life on a cross.

Again in the final moment of Carol Lee's life, I remembered saying to her, "Let go, it"s OK, go to God!" and immediately she "passed on." My prayers for her had been answered.

Dream # 19

THE CONFERENCE

November 8, 2008—4:00 AM

I'm traveling with a friend. We're in business suits in a car, and we arrive back at our hotel. It is obvious that a conference is what we are attending.

I go to our room, and Carol Lee is waiting for me dressed in a beautiful gown. She is standing in front of a dresser with a mirror and putting on her make-up.

She looks exceptionally beautiful (as she always did when we went to any event).

While I had already been dressed in a business suit and didn't have to change if I didn't want to, I suddenly see myself in "purple" (Carol Lee's favorite color) pajamas and in no way ready to go to the conference.

Carol Lee will now have to wait for me to change.

I wake up.

Carol Lee and I were never late for any event. We usually were the first to arrive and the last to leave—that is until she got sick.

Dream # 20

RETURN TO LIFE—
HAPPINESS IS HOLDING HANDS

November 14, 2008

Carol Lee and I are sitting in the backyard of our home (but it is not a home we ever lived in). I know (in the dream) that she has "passed on," but she has returned to me. I can't wait for our friends to come and join us. They won't believe she has returned.

The first to arrive is our pastor (again, not one I recognize from real life, but he looked like my first cousin once removed, Howie, who is a retired Presbyterian minister and who also participated in Carol Lee's memorial service at Abiding Peace Lutheran Church).

Carol Lee calls to me and says, "Pastor is at the front door, let him in." I go from the yard to the back door and through the house to the front door. I ask him to join us in the backyard. I have to step out the front door, and as Pastor comes in, he closes the door behind him, and the door locks, leaving me outside. I pound on the door, and he opens it. We go through the house and out the back door to join Carol Lee in the yard.

Soon, other friends join us (I didn't recognize any of them, but I knew they were friends). I was so proud that Carol Lee was there.

Soon, David joins us, and we start walking down the road. There is a carnival going on, and we are walking down the road between the rides and the shows.

Carol Lee and I are holding hands as we always did, and we are so very happy!

(In the last months of Carol Lee's life, we were paid a wonderful compliment by an elderly black woman. She said, "How great it is to see an elderly couple holding hands like a couple of teenagers.")

We pass a theater, and there is a long white bus in front of it. We say to each other that it must be the bus the movie stars used to get there. We pass one show and comment that David should not see it—it was too risqué.

We get to a building and go through the entrance and down the hallway. All of a sudden, Carol Lee's hand is so hot I can hardly hold it. I ask her if anything was wrong, being that she had returned from the dead. She says no, she is OK. But I know better. I know she is going to soon leave me again.

I wake up.

Dream # 21

OUR DREAM WEDDING

December 3, 2008—4:00 AM

Carol Lee and I are in a huge church. I'm in a tux, and Carol Lee is wearing a beautiful full skirt fuchsia gown. With her are six bridesmaids all in the same beautiful fuchsia gowns. Obviously, Carol Lee and I are getting married.

We join our guest and form a circle around the entire inside of the church—all holding hands. (Again Carol Lee and I are holding hands; annually, at our Sekula reunion on Labor Day, we all form a large circle and hold hands. We remember those who have passed on, and we release a white dove for each member of the family who has passed on since our last reunion. This past September, we released one for Carol Lee. A single white wing feather fell from the dove and was given to me. I placed it inside a picture frame containing a picture of Carol Lee, David, and me. Another white dove was released for my aunt Sophie who also passed on, ironically of the same disease—multiple myeloma cancer.)

When we get to the front of the church, at the altar, the wedding party separates from the rest of the guests who then sit down. The pastor then celebrates the Eucharist for Carol Lee and me. We eat the bread and drink the wine—the Body and Blood of our Lord and Savior, Jesus, the Christ.

DREAMS OF CAROL LEE

Oddly, we do not exchange the usual marriage vows. (In our view, God had put Carol Lee and me together for all eternity.)

After the Eucharist, I kiss Carol Lee, and we begin to leave the church.

It is a beautiful wedding.

Outside the church is the entire Lenape Valley High School Marching Band. They are going through their routine, playing one of their competition numbers. (I didn't recognize the tune, only that they were marching to it.)

We left the building and loaded onto a bus. (My family from Brandonville, Pennsylvania, hired a bus to travel from there to Aberdeen Proving Ground, Maryland, so that they could attend Carol Lee and my actual wedding at the Proving Ground Chapel; they did the same thing for David and Gina's wedding at Panther Valley in Hacketstown, New Jersey.) Presumably, the bus was taking us to our reception.

We have traveled quite a distance from the church. Suddenly, I realize we are traveling beside a beautiful trout stream in a wooded area. I am picking out likely spots in the stream where I could catch a trout.

We then come to a town, and the bus takes a right turn, crossing a bridge over the stream. It is a beautiful trout stream, and as we pass over it, I wake up.

Postscript:

When David was buying a home in New Hampshire, we had to travel to a neighboring town for him to sign the papers for his bank loan. The trip took us alongside a beautiful trout stream. While David was getting his loan, Carol Lee and I (hand in hand) walked down the street of the town looking in all the shops. At the end of the street, there was a bridge over the beautiful trout stream. We stopped so that I could admire it.

Dream # 22

A Tremendous Cook

December 9, 2008—2:00 AM

David and I were returning from a fishing trip. We had quit early, so Carol Lee wasn't expecting us until after dinner. We got out of the car and got on a three-wheel ATV. I drove the ATV directly up to our back porch. We went inside. Carol Lee was surprised to see us home. She was at the stove, cooking.

(Carol Lee was a tremendous cook. Several times within the last month, I commented on how I had gained twenty-five pounds on the first year of our marriage—from 150 pounds to 175 pounds. After we had each reached 209 pounds, we both went on a serious diet; Carol Lee and I both lost twenty-five pounds. I also commented that last Thanksgiving 2008, I was 180 pounds, only five pounds more than in 1964—after forty-four years of marriage to Carol Lee. I gained my usual four to five pounds at Thanksgiving, and I am trying to lose them before this Christmas. I know I'll gain another two to four pounds from Christmas to New Year. I'm now 184 pounds.)

Carol Lee was cooking for a friend she had invited over for dinner. The friend was sitting at the table. The table had been set for two. I did not recognize the friend. Presumably, she was a woman Carol Lee had worked with.

DREAMS OF CAROL LEE

(This past week, I had addressed my Christmas cards for 2008—my first time; Carol Lee had always addressed them in the past. There were several names of people I didn't recognize, most likely people Carol Lee had worked with. Somehow my subconscious mind created the face of a woman I had never seen in my entire life. I wonder if it was the face of someone Carol Lee had actually worked with. We will never know.)

I wake up.

Dream # 23

OUR FIRST MEETING

December 20, 2008—1:00 AM

I'm in the city trying to get home. I'm in my early twenties and by myself. I find myself in a very bad part of the city, but I have to cross from one side of the city to the other. I must cross through a Latino section. As I am walking down the street, I see a gang of six Latino boys. I must pass them, so I walk slowly on the other side of the street. I'm almost past them when one of them yells out, "Hey, white boy, what are you doing in our section of the city?" I don't answer, but keep walking. One of them picks up a stone and throws it at me. Another shoots a rock at me with a slingshot. The others start throwing stones at me. I see a brick and pick it up and throw it at them. This makes them more angry. One of them pulls out a knife and yells at me, "I have a knife, and I'm going to cut you." They begin to surround me. I make a break and run through a gap between them. The one with the knife throws it at me. I duck. It misses me, but hits one of his friends in the chest. He drops to the ground and someone yells, "Let's get out of here." We all run away.

I find myself running down a street that looks like the main street in Brandonville, Pennsylvania. I remember a store in the middle of the town where I would buy soda and ice cream. I go into the store, but there is a long line at the cashiers. So I don't get anything. I tell the cashier, "I would catch you later."

DREAMS OF CAROL LEE

I'm again walking down the street, and there is a crowd walking in the same direction. Suddenly, there is a beautiful young woman walking beside me. It is Carol Lee. She looks just the way she did when I first met her: beautiful with blonde hair. We walk together and begin talking. We both develop an immediate liking for one another and begin holding hands.

As we are walking down the street holding hands, a stray dog starts walking beside us.
(David's dogs: Bailey, who is older and almost black, always rested on my lap; and Bella, who is tan, always rested on Carol Lee's lap.) This dog was gray (like David's new dog Maizie) and frisky (like Maizie).

The dog begins running away, and Carol Lee asks me to go catch it and bring it back. I do so, but it runs away again. Again, I catch it and bring it back. This time, I find a rope and tie it to her collar. Carol Lee uses the rope as a leash for the dog.

We walk to the end of the town. There is a park at the end of the street and a bus stop at the end of the park. It is fall, and the leaves are on the ground. We walk through them. (This was something I always liked to do.)

When we get to the bus stop, I ask Carol Lee how she is getting home. She says she will call a girlfriend and ask her to pick her up. I say I will call one of my cousins.

I ask her what we are going to do with the dog. I suggest that she take the dog home with her, but if that doesn't work out, I will take it.

There is a small souvenir shop near the bus stop, and we go in to make our calls. As I pull the change out of my pocket to make my call, it falls among the souvenirs. I try to pick up the coins. There are Statues of Liberty, Empire State buildings, eagles, and other animals—all in pewter. The same color as the coins. I am afraid someone will say something to me for reaching for the coins among the souvenirs, but they don't.

We go back out to wait for our rides. I'm holding both of Carol Lee's hands and thinking how beautiful she is. We begin kissing. It is the sweetest, most wonderful kiss in both our lives. I say to myself, "She is the one I want to spend the rest of my life with." It is such a wonderful, sensuous kiss. I don't want it to stop. I realize that everyone is watching us kiss. I don't care. I don't want it to end.

Suddenly, Carol Lee's face begins to change. It becomes distorted—a face of an old woman—even as I am kissing her. She is hardly recognizable.

I wake up.

I'm lying there in bed, recollecting the dream. I'm puzzled by the ending. Then it hits me. She looked exactly the way she did when I last kissed her—moments after she had "passed on."

The wonderful moments when we were kissing were like the wonderful forty-four years of our wonderful, happy life spent together—the years being like seconds yet eternal. Had the dream continued before Carol Lee's sudden change, Carol Lee would have gone on to her home and I, to mine. The dog would have gone along with her. I think of it this way: The dog we both loved, Buttons, went on to heaven first. Carol Lee followed and is in God's hands in heaven. Someday, I will join Buttons and Carol Lee in heaven and continue the happiness we enjoyed during that sweet and wonderful kiss that we didn't want to end. This time, it won't. It will be for all eternity. It will never end.

Dream # 24

EAGLE SCOUT PROJECT

January 2, 2009—6:00 AM

I'm at a district scout meeting. One of the scoutmasters at the meeting informs me that one of the scouts in his troop is doing an Eagle project in front of my home, and he needs help. The next day, I see the scoutmaster and his scout working in a children's park in front of our house.

David is with me, and we go out to meet the scoutmaster. He informs me that the scout has been working all day with hardly a break. He then takes us to where the scout is working.

He is cleaning the area around a pond. The other scouts are clearing brush around the pond, but they can be there only for one day. We talk to the scout and explain to him that we live in the house directly in front of the park and are willing to help him.

As we look at the house, we see a beautiful "minimansion" or "minicastle" as we used to call them. We are walking on the path through the park toward the house, and I explain, "It's a beautiful park, too bad more children don't use it." Just then, two boys in a little electric car come down the path to the park. We continue on toward the house, and David gives the scout some refreshments that he had brought along.

EDWARD J. SEKULA, JR.

(David was always prepared—"Be Prepared.") He tells the scout that we will return that afternoon.

We leave the scout and his scoutmaster and return to our beautiful home. It has columns holding up the front porch like a typical Southern mansion. (Carol Lee had always wanted a home like this one—with Southern columns.)

Carol Lee is waiting on the porch for David and me to join her.

I wake up.

I like to believe that this is Carol Lee's "Southern mansion" in heaven. She is waiting there for David and me to someday join her. Someday, we will join her and be together through all eternity.

Earlier this same night, I once again heard Carol Lee call my name, "Ed."

During my tenure as scoutmaster of Troop 186 in Netcong, New Jersey, I had five scouts, including David, earn the rank of Eagle Scout. Carol Lee planned and directed their Eagle Courts of Honor and prepared an Eagle Scout memorial book for each one. The Morris-Sussex Council, BSA was so impressed that, for many years, they used her outline and memorial book as a guide for other troops holding Eagle Courts of Honor.

Dream # 25

CAROL LEE'S SURPRISE

January 6, 2009

Carol Lee and I are in a small compact house. (The only house similar that I lived in was during the years 1948-1957; we moved in with my grandfather when my grandmother died in 1957. I was a freshman at the Penn State University Pottsville campus.)

Friends of ours, a husband and wife familiar with the house, come to visit us. I offer them a drink and explain that we have a whole box of plastic cups in the closet. I go to the closet and open the door. The box of plastic cups is on the floor of the closet. Hanging on a rack in the closet are my military uniforms. (Obviously in the dream, I am still in the army. I spent two years in a small bachelor officer's quarter (BOQ) in the army at Aberdeen Proving Ground, where I met Carol Lee.) Except for my summer uniform, the rest are all khaki (but not like one I had ever owned). I am somewhat surprised. They are the modern desert tan camouflage khakis, and they are covered with spots of white sand (Middle East?).

I get the cups and show our friends another surprise that I discovered in the house. Next to the closet is a latch, and when you loosen it, which I did, a shelf comes down and forms a desk. On the top of the shelf, built into the wall, is a bookcase filled with all types of books. (It was almost exactly the same as my bookshelf in our downstairs "junk room" in Netcong; both Carol Lee and I loved to read.) I explain that the books were here when we moved into the house and that I didn't have time to go through them. Our friend's wife asks, "Was that three or four years ago?" I reply that it was more than five years ago.

She notices another latch on the wall just beyond the one that opens to the desk and bookshelf. Carol Lee and I had never opened it. She opens it, and to her and Carol Lee's surprise, it is a woman's dresser. There is a lighted mirror on the back of the wall. There is also a shelf that folded down.

Carol Lee is completely surprised and very happy to find it.

I wake up.

Dream # 26

FREEDOM AND HAPPINESS

January 12, 2009—4:00 AM

I'm dreaming that I am in bed sleeping. Suddenly, someone comes in the room and pulls the bedspread around me. Only my head is outside the bedspread. They tie a rope around me so that the only thing I can move is my head.

I'm frightened. Who did this? What did they want? Were they going to rob me? Was this another one of my nightmare dreams?

Suddenly, I see someone run up the hallway like they are chasing someone. They turn and run up the hallway in the opposite direction.

It's Carol Lee!

She comes into the bedroom and unties me and tells me that they are gone. (She had chased them away).

After she unties me, we lay down on the bed, and I give her a great big hug (thanking her). We start kissing.

I look around the room, and I see Debbie, Lisa, and Kara (her nieces).

I have a very happy and wonderful feeling.

I wake up.

Carol Lee's illness had almost totally constrained us. We were limited in what we could do. She felt badly that I was so constrained (as if I were tied up). Her "passing on" had freed me. In this dream, she reminded me that she was still watching over me—my guardian angel—and that I could still hug and kiss her in my dreams. She also reminded me that her family was still here to be with me.

Dream # 27

TROUT FISHING

January 18, 2009—5:00 AM

Carol Lee and I are driving down the road. We stop the car and get out. Something, (I don't know what) a parade or something else causes us to stop.

There is a trout stream between us and a road on the other side of the stream. Something is about to happen on that road. We walk up along the stream to get a better view.

There is a little hill a short distance up the stream but we would have to wade through a knee-deep little bay to get to it. I look in the water and see a snake about fifteen or twenty feet long. I think only an anaconda or python gets that large. (Carol Lee was always deathly afraid of snakes; she didn't like being around them.) I know that they, like most wild animals, are as afraid of you as you are of them. I step into the water without taking off either my shoes or socks. Immediately, the snake slithers off into the deeper water and disappears.

I come back for Carol Lee. She is wearing a dress that comes down only to her knees. She takes her shoes off and holds them in one hand. I take her other hand, and we wade across the little bay area. We climb the hill; and as we get to the top where we are going to sit to watch whatever is going to take place, looking across the hill to the other side, I notice the tips of two fly rods sticking up in the air. I don't have my fly rods with me, but I had fished that spot many times. There is a fisherman on the other side of the hill. I talk with him and tell him that I had caught several trout in the riffle coming into the pool below the hill Carol Lee and I are sitting on, several across from us and several downstream at the end of the pool.

I wake up.

Carol Lee had gone trout fishing with me in Pennsylvania at Fishing Creek near Bloomsburg. One spot I had fished was very similar to the one in the dream. The stream was below a small hill, and you had to climb down the hill to get to it. Carol Lee sat at the top of the hill to watch me fish. I had to wade across the stream and fish back toward Carol Lee from the other side. I caught a trout in the riffle directly across from where she was sitting. I had caught another one at the end of the pool but not the day she was watching me. Just below the end of the pool was a steel bridge where the road crossed over the stream. Below the steel bridge was another riffle and pool. These had been our favorite fishing spots—especially for Dad, Mom, Al (Yeninas), and me. Over the middle of the pool was one of the last old wooden bridges on Fishing Creek and in that section of Pennsylvania. This stretch of stream, especially the riffle, was one of my all-time favorite spots to fish. I had probably caught more trout in this stretch than anywhere else in Pennsylvania. There are two spots in New Jersey where I had caught more trout.

There was an old one-room school, like the two I had attended grade school (first to third and fourth to sixth grades) at the end of the wooden bridge. The bridge had long since been closed to traffic, and you can now only walk across it. We had always parked our car near the school and walked up the stream to begin fishing. The day Carol Lee was with us, we had parked here and walked up along the stream crossed over the road and up to the hill where she sat and watched me fish.

What a wonderful dream of remembrance.

DREAMS OF CAROL LEE

Surprisingly, yesterday I was fishing in a pool directly across from our condo at Orange Lake in Florida. Ken, Liz, and I were spending a month's vacation in Florida. I met a fisherman there, and we spent over an hour trading fishing stories. He was from West Virginia, and I told him Carol Lee was born in West Virginia. He asked where, and I told him Mount Hope. He said, "Oh, that's near Beckley." He had lived near there and had grown up there—small world.

Dream # 28

WALKING ON WATER

January 31, 2009—5:00 AM
(Super Bowl Sunday)

I awake from a deep sleep. I had several inconsequential dreams, none of which were worth recording.

I'm lying on the bed in a state of semiconsciousness, trying to get back to sleep. My mind is going over the previous day and the fisherman I met who was staying in the condo next to ours. (Liz, Ken, and I are staying in a condo in a section of Orange Lake that Carol Lee and I had never stayed before.) There is a fishing pond right behind our condo, but the fisherman told me the pond above that one was a better one to fish in.

My mind was anticipating fishing the pond above ours, but then went on to the one near the condo that I own. Last week, when we were staying in my condo, I went fishing in that pond. The pond had been stocked with fish, and the fish were swimming in a school and circling round the pond. Each time they passed by where I was fishing, I would cast my lure into the middle of the school, but none of them would hit my lure. I didn't catch any of them.

Without realizing it, I slipped from my semiconscious state to a dream state. I am still at the pond.

Suddenly, for no reason at all, I look out over the pond. There is Carol Lee, standing on the water. She is glowing with a radiant light like an angel. She is my guardian angel.

I wake up to full consciousness.

What is amazing is the fact that I slipped from semiconsciousness to dream state without my mind moving from the pond. Let the experts explain it.

I know and believe that only my Lord and Savior, Jesus, the Christ, walked on water.
To dream that Carol Lee also walked on water is also truly amazing.

Dream # 29

Bird Costume

February 7, 2009—2:00 AM

Carol Lee is dressed in a bird costume she had made. (Of all the costumes she had made, she never had made a bird costume.)

She is wearing big orange bird feet that came up to her knees. She is also wearing a bird's head mask with a large yellow beak.

Carol Lee is at a table, handing out cookies and pieces of cake that she had baked for a crowd of people or anyone who is walking by.

I run to get my new digital camera (I actually had purchased a new digital camera shortly after Carol Lee had passed on) and try to take a picture of her, but I can't get the camera in focus. It keeps blinking or would zoom in and out. She tells me to take the pictures anyway; they will come out fine.

I begin taking pictures of Carol Lee and all the people in front of her table. She takes her bird mask off so I can get a better picture of her. Soon, there are over a dozen people standing around Carol Lee, with her in the middle.

As I'm taking the pictures, I wish I can be in the picture with her and with them.

DREAMS OF CAROL LEE

I wake up.

I guess I'm still wishing I could be with my beloved Carol Lee.

Jesus said, "I am the resurrection and the life." Someday, I will again be with my beloved Carol Lee in heaven for all eternity.

Dream # 30

WATCHING OVER ME—II

February 21, 2009—11:00 PM

Almost every night, I watch TV sitting on our love seat recliner. I have a tendency to fall asleep during a commercial, which I "tune out" mentally instead of watching. I'm usually semiprone in the recliner.

I fall asleep and begin dreaming that I'm watching TV. I'm semiprone in the recliner (which at that moment, I actually am, but it is a different recliner).

Suddenly, Carol Lee comes up to me. She adjusts the recliner so that I am sitting upright. She says, "You'll be more comfortable sitting upright than being semiprone."
She then pushes the recliner about ten feet closer to the TV and says, "You'll be able to see the TV better now." I feel more comfortable and can see the TV much better.

I wake up.

Carol Lee, my guardian angel, is telling me she is still looking after me. She is trying to make my life without her more comfortable and is helping me to see my continued journey here on earth. I know she will be with me until I "pass on". Then we will be one again, be rejoined in the presence of God (heaven as we call it) for all eternity.

Dream # 31

ADVICE ON HOW TO HELP SOMEONE

February 24, 2009—2:00 AM
(Shrove Tuesday)

I'm in the hospital at the bedside of a female patient. (I don't know why I am there.)

There are two nurses assisting the patient. She is having a great deal of trouble, and the nurses are not quite sure what they should do. The patient goes into convulsion, and the nurses attending to her don't know what to do. They have been discussing what type of bandage they should put on the patient.

I leave the room and meet Carol Lee. I tell her what is happening. She suggests that they use a "belly bandage," one that covers her entire abdominal area.

I go back in to the patient's bedside. The nurses had calmed the patient down and are again discussing what to do. I tell them my wife, Carol Lee, suggests that they use a belly bandage. She had used it before, and it worked well for her in a similar situation.

I wake up.

In the dream, Carol Lee was advising me on how to help someone else. I'm in the process of writing a book covering the lives of both Carol Lee and myself, *Carol Lee and Ed, A Beautiful Life*. It is my hope that Carol Lee's six-year fight with multiple myeloma cancer may help other people fight that or a similar cancer.

Dream # 32

Two New Puppies

February 24, 2009—10:00 pm

I'm watching the president's speech on TV. I'm beginning to fade in and out of sleep. Once again, I fall completely asleep, but I'm still watching the president's speech.

I begin to get worried. Carol Lee isn't home yet. What has happened to her? Where can she be?

Suddenly, I hear a noise upstairs. I become afraid. I call out, "Carol Lee, is that you?"
I get no answer.

Slowly I start up the stairs to see who or what is making the noise. It's a little puppy.
It is running around the upstairs railing. As I get to the top of the stairs, it comes running to me. I look around and see another puppy in the living room.

Again, I call out, "Carol Lee," but again no answer. I go to the bedroom, and there she is, lying on the bed sound asleep. I wake her up and ask her when she got home. I didn't hear her come in. She wakes up and smiles at me. She had bought two puppies and came home and went directly to bed.

EDWARD J. SEKULA, JR.

I am so happy that she is home safe, and I can see and talk with her.

I wake up.

Carol Lee still makes me happy. We talked about replacing our dog, Buttons, but because of her health and the traveling we did, we decided not to. She may have been suggesting that I purchase one or two puppies to keep me company, but I'm still traveling too much to properly take care of them. Maybe later when health reasons forces me to slow down.

Dream # 33

Marching Band Competition

March 3, 2009—2:00 AM

This dream is quite vague. I didn't wake up at the end of the dream as I usually do. Instead of waking up, I continued into another dream and then another.

Carol Lee and I are in a building where a concert is being held. (I assume it is Abiding Peace Lutheran Church in Budd Lake.)

Outside the building is the Mt. Olive Marching Band in their brilliant red and gold uniforms. The tuba line of the band is pressed almost against the windows of the building. The rest of the marching band is directly behind them.

At a certain point in the concert, they are to join in and add their music to that of the concert going on inside.

Behind the Mt. Olive Marching Band is the Lenape Valley Patriots Marching Band in their red, white, and blue uniforms. I am thinking, *This is just like one of the many band competitions that Carol Lee and I attended.*

From here, the dream becomes vague.

EDWARD J. SEKULA, JR.

I find myself in another fishing dream with my cousin, John.

I finally wake up.

The four years of our life, when David was in high school and a member of the Lenape Valley Patriots Marching Band, were among the best years of our lives. Carol Lee was treasurer of the band, and I was the unofficial assistant treasurer. We traveled to many band competitions and trips over these four years and where Carol Lee and I served as band chaperone. The marching band won many trophies during these years, and in David's senior year (1984, the band's greatest year ever), it achieved a third-place standing among all the marching bands in its class on the East Coast. David would go on to place second in the state of New Jersey on his instrument, the barry saxophone. He was invited to a special band performance at St. Mary's in Virginia at the northeastern most tip of the Chesapeake Bay. What a view of the ocean from there. There, Carol Lee and I were entertained at a fabulous rehearsal and concert. Next, David would be invited to perform a concert tour in nine European countries with Youth of America. What a wonderful way for David to end his high school years. You can't imagine what proud parents Carol Lee and I were. What a year.

Dream # 34

MEETING IN HEAVEN

March 5, 2009—2:00 AM

I'm home alone. It's not a home I recognize. Suddenly, I hear a noise and become scared. Carol Lee is not with me. She had gone somewhere and wouldn't be home until much later. I hear the noise again, and I'm afraid someone has broken into our house.

I call out, "Who's there?" but there is no answer. I call out again, "Carol Lee, is that you?" Still no answer.

I slowly begin moving through the house. In the living room is a spiral staircase. Halfway up, I see Carol Lee. She is wearing a beautiful gown and looking more beautiful and radiant than I had ever seen her. I ask her why she was home so early. She says she had finished what she was doing much earlier than she had expected, and so she came home.

She goes upstairs, and I also go up to greet her. I hug her and tell her how glad I am to see her. We begin kissing. It is the most passionate kiss we had ever had.

I wake up.

EDWARD J. SEKULA, JR.

I believe Carol Lee was standing on the stairway to heaven. She got there first, earlier than either of us had expected and earlier than she should have. I follow her (sometime in the future). Our meeting and the way we will spend eternity together will be beautiful.

Jesus is the stairway to heaven.

Dream # 35

FALLING ASLEEP AT THE WHEEL

March 20, 2009—6:30 AM

Carol Lee and I are traveling on the New Jersey turnpike. As usual, the traffic is extremely heavy. Oddly, I am driving from the backseat. There is a steering wheel on the passenger side of the backseat of the car. A car cuts us off, followed by another car.

Carol Lee says, "It looks like the one car is chasing the other." I tell her that I shouldn't be driving from the backseat; it is too dangerous and that she should take over.

She is sitting in the front seat behind the steering wheel, and she begins driving. Again, oddly, I am not looking through my eyes but through Carol Lee's. I am looking at people walking beside the road instead of looking at the highway. I start calling her name, "Carol Lee, Carol Lee," but there is no response. I'm afraid we are going to crash. I still can't see the road, only the people walking beside the road. Again I call, "Carol Lee, Carol Lee." She wakes up just in time to stop for a toll booth. I ask her, "What happened?" She responds, "I don't know. I must have fallen asleep."

I wake up.

When I first saw Carol Lee on January 27, 2008, in her hospital bed just several hours before she "passed on," she was sleeping. After kissing her on the cheek, I put my hand on her forehead and asked, "What happened to you?" I did not expect an answer. She turned her head toward me, opened her eyes, and said, "I don't know." These were her last words. She turned her head back and closed her eyes, never to open them again.

The toll booth could be the "gateway to heaven." I was thinking about it in our discussion at our "Sharing the Faith" session conducted by Pastor Becky Thane, our pastor at Abiding Peace Lutheran Church. Also I was sorting my folders on the table in our dining room. One folder was "Dreams," containing a draft of this book through the dream just previous to this one. On the inside of the cover of this folder is a picture of Carol Lee's "gateway to heaven"—the platform on signal rock on the southern peak of the Massanutten Mountain in Virginia. The "gateway" is used by hang gliders who jump off the end of the platform and sore over the beautiful Shenandoah Valley. It is built of the historical rock outcrop where the Confederate general Stonewall Jackson had placed his signal officer to observe the movement of the two Union Armies trying to trap him between them.

In real life as opposed to dreams, I could relate to two incidents involving driving. In one, I was driving to a Rotary conference when my allergies caused me to go into a sneezing fit. It seemed I would never stop. I do stop but only because I had sneezed so hard I passed out. Carol Lee kept yelling my name, "Ed, Ed, Ed, Ed." I began drifting into oncoming traffic. Because of her continuously calling my name, I finally regained consciousness, just in time to avoid the oncoming traffic. I was in the wrong lane. We had just narrowly avoided a head-on collision. God must have been with us that day.

The other incident was when we were driving north on Interstate 91. We were going to David's home in New Hampshire. We had just eaten brunch (breakfast for me) and lunch for Carol Lee at the Cracker Barrel in Holyoke, Massachusetts. Generally, I would get a little sleepy after eating, so Carol Lee would take over the driving responsibilities for the rest of the trip. I almost fell asleep when I heard a loud noise. I woke up and asked what had happened. Carol Lee said she must have fallen asleep. Our van was drifting into the passing lane just as a pickup truck was passing us. Fortunately, only our side view mirrors collided, which was the loud noise I had heard. The noise woke us both up.

Carol Lee was so shaken up that she could hardly drive to next exit where we could switch drivers. She would never drive on an Interstate or turnpike again. Once again, as in many times in our lives, God must have been with us.

Dream # 36

SEARCHING FOR A DOG

March 22, 2009—2:30 AM

This was a long, rambling dream. I only have vague memories of its beginning.

We are at an event on a farm. There are many dignitaries at the event. David is with us. After dinner and dancing, David and I begin walking around the farm. We are searching for a dog to purchase. I don't see anyone I know. We go from building to building. There are many buildings. (In real life, this reminded me of when I was a boy and we went to the Bloomsburg fair in Pennsylvania.) Each contains exceptionally large vegetables, especially the one with red radishes and pumpkins. We can see dogs running around, but no one to ask about them.

In one of the buildings, we find a stand that is selling food and other items. I tell David, "Someone here should be able to help us."

At that moment, Carol Lee joins us. She is young—late twenties or early thirties. She is wearing a beautiful gown. (She always did at the events we went to.) She is radiant, the most beautiful I had ever seen her. I give her a kiss on the cheek and a great big hug. David joins us and hugs his mother. Carol Lee asks me to tell David that he is hugging her too hard. I respond, "You tell him."

DREAMS OF CAROL LEE

I wake up.

Carol Lee, David, and I had visited many wineries when we were on our vacations. Most of them were on a farm. This past Thursday at Rotary, I was paying the owner of the Bella Vita where we eat lunch. We were in the kitchen, and she showed me some of the very large red peppers she had just received. They were the largest either of us had ever seen.

Everyone thinks I should get a dog, which may account for David and me trying to buy a dog from the farmer in the dream.

Carol Lee's passing greatly affected David. The two of them were very close.

Yesterday, I completed my listing of Carol Lee's entries in her calendar/journal from 1985 to her last entry on January 13, 2008. In exactly six months from her last entry, we would have celebrated our forty-fifth anniversary. As a postscript, I drafted what would probably be the last chapter in my autobiography and Carol Lee's biography, *Carol Lee and Ed, A Beautiful Life*.

Dream # 37

The Pattern

April 10, 2009—4:00 AM

Again, I'm dreaming that I am sleeping. I was not in our Netcong home but in another smaller house, similar to some of the vacation condos we stayed in. We are not on vacation. We are living in the small home.

I hear a noise downstairs, and I wake up (in my dream). I get out of bed and go to the staircase. Carol Lee appears and asks me what I was doing up. I should be sleeping. I tell her I had heard someone talking. Carol Lee was talking with a friend. Spread out on the floor was material for pattern, waiting for her to cut it out. (Carol Lee and her favorite hobby—making doll clothes for American Girl Dolls; she had five dolls.) I didn't recognize the friend. Carol Lee says we had to go back to the old house to get her sewing machine. That was the end of the dream.

Instead of waking up immediately, I simply fell into a deeper sleep. I didn't wake up until almost 6:30. I really don't know the significance of this dream, only that Carol Lee was there, and I talked with her. One of the saddest days in Carol Lee's life was when her fingers became too stiff to sew, and she had to give up making her doll dresses.

I had just returned from almost a week at David's in New Hampshire. He was recovering from his stomach operation and had lost over one hundred pounds.

Dream # 38

A Bleeding Foot

April 23, 2009—5:00 AM

In the dream, David is very young. He is just able to walk. He is playing with one of his cousins when he yells out. I ask what happened. His cousin replies that David had stepped on a nail. David has begun walking toward me. As he walks, he is leaving bloody footprints. I realize that it is bad. I grab his foot and put my thumb on the wound and apply pressure. This should have stopped the bleeding, but it does not. I become anxious, almost panicking, as the blood continues to spurt out.

I yell to Carol Lee who is lying in her bed, "Get me some cotton." She jumps out of bed and goes to the closet where we keep the cotton and other bandages. She brings the cotton to me. I apply the cotton to the wound and stop the bleeding.

I wake up.

When David was about the same age as he was in the dream, he was jumping on a bed in his aunt Liz's house in Maryland. He fell and struck his head against the bedpost, causing a cut just under his eye. We tried to stop the bleeding, but had to rush him to the emergency room of the hospital at Havre De Grace. It took two stitches to stop the bleeding.

EDWARD J. SEKULA, JR.

The time I panicked most was when Carol Lee's cancer began coming back after her transplant. Her nose began to bleed, and we could not stop it. Her white cell count was too low. I had to rush her to the emergency room of Morristown General Hospital where they packed her nose with cotton and stopped the bleeding. They showed us how to apply pressure on the nose to help. This began happening frequently, but each time, we packed her nose with cotton and applied pressure as they had shown us. Each time, we were able to stop the bleeding. Eventually, Carol Lee was able to stop the bleeding herself. When her blood count was low, we had to be especially careful that she didn't cut herself. However, there was no way to prevent her nose from bleeding. These nosebleeds became a sign of the continued advancement of her cancer.

Dream # 39

TRIP TO PENN STATE

April 27, 2009—5:00 AM

Carol Lee and I are driving toward Penn State. We are headed directly for Ole Maine, which, with its many columns, looks somewhat like the Capitol building in Washington DC (This dream is similar to an earlier dream).

As we get close, I turn to the right to go to the building we wanted to visit. Suddenly, I realize that I should have turned left instead of right. There are no places for us to turn around, and I have to keep going. I explain to Carol Lee that Penn State extends way out even to where we are now driving. It is a narrow road on a hillside. (This road or hillside does not exist at Penn State.)

Finally, I find a turn to the left. I go up a hill to a gasoline station and turn around. For some unknown reason, I stop at a bank on the corner. I park the car on the street in front of the bank, thinking it should only take me a minute to run into the bank. There are not that many cars driving on the street at the time. I'm coming out of the bank when, for some reason (perhaps I forgot something), I turn around and go back into the bank. I notice a car directly behind ours, wanting for us to move.

When I do come outside, our car isn't there. I realize that Carol Lee must have shifted over to the driver's side and pulled out to let the car behind us go. I know she will go around the block and pick me up. She does, stops the car, and I get in. We still couldn't turn around, so Carol Lee has to continue driving. Coming down a hill we spot a U-turn, but Carol Lee is going too fast. As she is turning, our momentum carries us up over the curb and into the woods. I ask, "Did we damage anything?" She replies, "Only a few scratches on the side of the car." I say I didn't care about a few scratches.

Carol Lee tries to back out of the woods, but the car doesn't move. I'm afraid we damaged the transmission or something else. But she says, "Oh! I know what is the matter." She had placed the gear shift into neutral instead of reverse. She puts the gear in reverse and backs out onto the highway. We are finally on the right road headed in the right direction.

Carol Lee remarks, "You know, when I was seventeen years old, I received this award. I was the only one in the whole area to receive it. If the organization still existed, maybe we could contact them." I say, "That was over fifty years ago, I doubt if they're still in existence." She says, "They have changed their name, but were still in existence."

I wake up.

At seventeen, Carol Lee belonged to an exclusive group of young women called the Rainbow Girls. She had received a very high award from them.

She also received, posthumously, Rotary International's Fellowship Award from the Wallkill Valley Rotary Club.

Dream # 40

ANOTHER HUG AND KISS

May 8, 2009—11:30 PM

I'm watching TV and fall asleep.

There is Carol Lee sitting behind the piano. She looks so beautiful! I go to her, and she gets up and comes out from behind the piano. We hug and begin kissing. It is a long, beautiful kiss. Everything is so wonderful. We are together again. This is how heaven must feel like.

I wake up.

God, how I still miss her.

Someday, this dream will become a reality, when once again I can hug and kiss her in heaven.

Dream # 41

REALITY AND THE SUBCONSCIOUS

July 3, 2009—11:00 PM

In this dream, reality and my subconscious become somewhat fused.

I am watching TV. I fall asleep and begin dreaming that I am watching TV. Suddenly, I hear Carol Lee calling me from upstairs. I try to wake up to respond to her, but I can't. I keep drifting back into a deep sleep. Again, Carol Lee calls me and asks me to put our dog, Buttons, outside. Again, I try to wake up but can't. Again, she calls. This time I wake up enough to get up from the couch where I was watching TV and sleeping. I head toward the staircase, but I'm still half asleep and walk into the wall. Again, Carol Lee calls me, stating that Buttons really needs to go out. This time, I make it up the stairs to landing at the door. Carol Lee is standing at the top of the steps, and Buttons makes a dash to me on the landing. I open the door and let her out.

I wake up.

One possible interpretation of this dream is that Carol Lee and Buttons are in heaven, and Carol Lee is calling me to join them. Or that this life on earth is really a dream from which I have not yet wakened—I'm still asleep. The reality is heaven and Carol Lee and Buttons are waiting for me and calling me to come to them).

Dream # 42

THE PERFECT SON

July 11, 2009—4:00 AM

It's Thanksgiving in Maryland at Carol Lee's sister Liz's home. Carol Lee's nieces—Debbie, Lisa, and Kara—and our son, David, are playing cards, laughing, telling jokes and stories. (They do this every Thanksgiving when they get together.) Lisa is telling a story about a friend who has a problem that the doctors can't cure. David tells her to have her friend take (something) which should help relieve the problem.

Suddenly, Carol Lee and I are back home in New Jersey. Carol Lee comes to me crying.
I ask her what is wrong. She says she just had a call from Lisa. Her friend did what David told Lisa to tell her to do. She did, but became deathly sick. They don't know if she would live or die. Lisa says that what David said her friend should do was totally wrong.

Carol Lee couldn't control her crying. I go to her and hug her, trying to help her control her crying, but it doesn't help.

I ask her what was the worst they could do, "Sue David?" I ask her, "Did they threaten to sue?" She says, "Yes," and continues to cry.

I tell her that whatever happens, we could deal with it.

EDWARD J. SEKULA, JR.

I woke up.

David was always the "apple of her eye." He could do no wrong. He was the gentlest, warmest, kindest, and most honest person she had ever known. He was the perfect son.

Dream # 43

KEYS TO THE DOORWAY TO HEAVEN

July 19, 2009—5:00 AM

Carol Lee, David, and I are returning home from somewhere. I take my keys out of my pocket. The key is on a little chain. I take the key and open the screen door.

(At the time of this dream, I was staying at my aunt Anna's in Brandonville, Pennsylvania, overnight. When I got there, she had given me a key to her front door. It was on a little chain.)

I open the screen door and unlocked our regular door to our home, but the screen door closes behind me.

Carol Lee begins fussing at me and reaches for the key in her pocketbook, thinking the screen door had locked itself behind me. I turned to her and said, "For christ's sake, quit fussing at me. The screen door is still open."

I wake up.

While this was an inappropriate use of our Lord's name, it reminds me of "On account of Christ" in the "Apology to the Augsburg Confession" in the *Book of Concord*, which I am studying. "On

EDWARD J. SEKULA, JR.

account of Christ, our sins are forgiven." This is a constant theme in the "Apology" and the heart of Lutheran theology. Christ has "opened the door" to heaven. He is the "doorway to heaven." All we have to do is to have faith and believe in him.

Dream # 44

TRAVEL ADVENTURE

July 25, 2009—12:15 AM

The dream begins with Carol Lee and me, driving down the road in our "new" car. It is another one of our travel adventures or "road trip" as Carol Lee and I used to call them.

Suddenly, it gets so foggy that I can't see the road. I don't know if I am on the road or off it. I slowly step on the brake and come to a stop. Carol Lee tells me to turn on the lights.

I fumble around looking for the light switch and finally find it. Since it is a new car, I'm still not familiar with the location of all the controls on the dashboard.

With the lights on, we can see the road again, so I start driving. We are headed toward a mountain range, and the road turns into a dirt road. The dirt road gets worse until it is no longer a road, but becomes a dirt trail. We come to a stream, and there is no way to go but to drive down the stream. It is a shallow stream, so I begin driving down the stream. I look for a place where I can get out of the stream and drive on dry land. The water gets deeper and deeper, but still there is nowhere to drive up and out of the stream. There are now rocks in the stream, and I must drive around them. We get caught in a deep current, but I realize the car is floating. We keep traveling down the stream until it joins a river.

(White River Junction in Vermont where the White River joins Connecticut—our exit off Interstate 91 and onto Interstate 89 on our way to David's in New Hampshire.)

There is a sandy beach where the stream joins the river. I drive up and onto it.

Suddenly, our car is no longer a car. It is a large electric scooter. (I purchased a large battery-powered scooter for Carol Lee in May of 2007.) The scooter had an elongated body with a driver's seat for me and another one behind it for Carol Lee. I stop the scooter, and we get off. The beach had eroded, and there is a four-foot drop-off to the river. (This is similar to the beach erosion at Ocean City, Maryland, where we vacationed for many years prior to the beach restoration project for the Ocean City beaches.) I try to climb up from the river, but as I get near the top, the sand gives way, and I slide back down to the river. I try again to climb up the bank, but again, the sand gives way, and I slide back down.

A forest ranger (park ranger) appears and calls out my name, "Mr. Sekula." I answer yes and ask him how he knew my name. The ranger says he knew the name of everyone who passed this way. I was going to ask him to help me get up the sandy embankment, when I realize that if Carol Lee and I go back to where the steam and the river joined, we could follow the trail I had taken with the scooter.

Carol Lee and I get back on the scooter and begin up the trail leading from the river. I ask her if she brought my fishing tackle and she answers yes. I turn and see my tackle box, rod, and reel near her in the back of the scooter.

As we are driving down the trail along the river, we come to other people with scooters. In the center of one of parked scooters is a table setup, a fly tying vise, and all the material to make deer hair bass bugs. Several newly tied bass bugs are on the table near the vise. Then I notice an umbrella type device which had a bass bug attached to it. It has a leader attached to one of the ribs of the umbrella. These are very different types of bass bugs. I had never seen any like them. I knew their design might entice a bass to "hit" one of them. They are also made out of brightly colored dyed deer hair with silver and gold tinsel extending from the body of the bass bugs, looking like shiny legs. I notice that they were for sale, and I almost buy one. Then I realize I could tie one exactly the same when we got home.

We start out again and reach a small town. There is an auction going on with all types of fishing clothes and hats. I spot a fishing cap which I really like, but then I realize I am already wearing a weird cap. It is more like a hood than a cap and hung down to my shoulders. I take it off and find that I am already wearing a fishing cap underneath the hood. I don't need to buy another fishing cap.

(Since Carol Lee passed on, my fishing buddy, Pat, and I go to Cabela's near Reading, Pennsylvania, to buy fishing lines and lures for our annual fishing trip to Maine. This past year was our twenty-first consecutive fishing trip. Pat almost always buys a new T-shirt, but this past year, he bought a fishing hat like the one both David and I wear.)

As I'm walking back to the scooter, I find a whole line of scooters. They are for sale at bargain prices.

Suddenly, my father, Ed Sr., is walking beside me. We look for Carol Lee and our scooter, but can't find it. We keep walking down the trail away from the little town. Finally, we see Carol Lee driving the scooter ahead of us. We run to catch up to her. I ask her why she drove away without us. She replies, "I don't know." (Her very last word on this planet earth.)

I wake up.

One could interpret this as a travel adventure in heaven. There are many indications, especially meeting and walking with my father, but I'll let you interpret it.

Dream # 45

BIG TROUT

July 28, 2009—2:00 AM

Carol Lee and I are riding in the backseat of someone's car. I don't recognize who is driving or who is sitting beside him (presumably friends of ours). The road comes alongside a beautiful trout stream. I start looking out the window to see if I can spot a trout in the stream. I do. It is an extremely large trout. I estimate its length to be thirty inches long.

The driver stops the car, and we all get out. Standing at the railing beside the road, I try to point out where the large trout was in the stream, but it had moved. I can't see it. Where could it have gone? Then I notice the stream had washed out the ground under the embankment on the other side of the stream. Sure enough, I could now get a glimpse of the trout's nose or tail every now and then as it moved. Neither Carol Lee or the couple with us could see it.

I wake up.

The largest trout I had ever caught measured twenty-three inches. I caught it when I was in my teens at Fisherman's Paradise on Spring Creek just west of Belefonte, Pennsylvania, and just east of the Pennsylvania State University where I would attend college and get to fish here again when I was in my twenties. We stayed at Trout Inn in Belefonte where

Spring Creek ran along the road on the other side of the street. Crossing the street, you came to a railing protecting you from falling down a walled embankment into the stream. When you looked down from the railing, you could see many large trout in the 20" to 30" range. I always looked forward to staying at Trout Inn and crossing the street to see the large trout.

Also when I was in my teens, in the fall of the year, the large trout from the Pumping Station Dam near Brandonville, Pennsylvania, went into the tributaries to the dam to spawn. In these small tributaries, they would always hide from us in the undercuts of the embankment so we could not see them.

Dream # 46

SHORT VISIT

July 28, 2009—4:00 AM

Carol Lee visits me twice in the same night.

After dreaming about the "Big Trout" and several other dreams, which I floated in and out of, I dream I'm tired, and I lie down on the bed.

Suddenly, Carol Lee comes and joins me. She lies down on the other side of the bed. We begin talking (but I can't remember what we talked about). In my dream, I realize that this must be a dream. Carol Lee can't be here with me; she has "passed on."

I wake up.

Even though this was one of the shortest of my dreams, it was a wonderful moment of being with her once again and being able to talk to her, even if it was only for a moment.

Dream # 47

Doing Good

July 29, 2009—2:30 AM

Carol Lee and I are at a mall. We sit down on a bench. She is going through her pocketbook, looking for a piece of paper with a name on it. She has many pieces of paper with names and addresses and other information on them, but she can't find the one she is looking for. A folded piece of paper drops to the floor. Carol Lee picks it up and unwraps it. Wrapped in the folded piece of paper are several $10 bills.

She becomes very concerned. It is money we had collected in Summit, New Jersey, and had not given it to the charity for which we collected it. She becomes more concerned that we could no longer use it for the cause intended.

I look around the mall and see that we are near an ice cream stand. I want to get an ice cream cone for Carol Lee and myself. Then I realize that we are not allowed to have ice cream (we both had diabetes).

Carol Lee is still very upset. I tell her not to worry about the money. We can give it to our congregation, Abiding Peace Lutheran Church or another charity. We give to many charities. This eases Carol Lee's mind, and she feels so good she did something weird. She lies down on the floor of the mall and begins thrashing her hands and feet. To my amazement, everyone in the mall begins doing the same.

EDWARD J. SEKULA, JR.

I wake up.

If you do something good, others will follow you and do the same. For many years, we have contributed quarterly to many charities including many Native American schools and other needs and causes:

St. Joseph's Indian School
Southwest Indian Fund
Red Cloud Indian School
St. Labre Indian School
St. Francis Mission (Native American)
Council of Indian Nations
American Indian Relief Fund
Native American Relief Fund
Navajo Relief Fund
Running Strong for American Indian Youth
American Indian Education Fund

And many other charities such as Feed the Hungry, Boys Town, Feed the Children, etc.

We also give quarterly to the Christian Appalachian Project. Some of our poorest people try to survive in Appalachia: Kentucky, Tennessee, and West Virginia. Carol Lee was born in West Virginia, and our contributions were a small way of trying to help.

Yesterday, I received my weekly telephone call from my son, David. Among the things we talked about was our Rotary BBQ this past Saturday. I told him I bought a dozen of corn, but since I could use only two ears of corn, I took the rest to church (Abiding Peace Lutheran Church) and shared them with the rest of our congregation. He said we should start a "sharing table" where people can bring in excess vegetables that had grown and share them with others. I said that we had already begun doing exactly that but had not formalized the process or gotten others to do the same. However, like Carol Lee in the dream, if you do good, others will follow you.

Dream # 48

THE PARTY

August 3, 2009—6:00 AM

Carol Lee and I are at a party. We're in a very large room filled with people. We're sitting at a table where there are all kinds of food and drinks. Mom and Dad (Dorothy and Ed Sr.) are sitting with us. (Carol Lee and I once took Mom and Dad to a Polka Festival at Great Gorge in northern New Jersey.) We are having a wonderful time. Everyone is very happy.

The party begins to break up and people start leaving. Jo Anne (Kehley/Morabito) and Andy appear at our table and say that the whole Kehley family are over at the other end of the room. I go over and sure enough all of the Kehleys are there. Cliff and the boys (men) greet me. I'm surprised; Cliff looks as young as the boys. They actually appear to be the same age. I think Carol Lee had never met Cliff when he was that young. When she first met him, we were already calling him the Grey Eagle. Buddy (Clifford) and Helen and Lois and Joe are also there, and I greet them. When I get to their table, Mae is sitting there, and I say to her I need to go back to our table and bring Carol Lee over so she could see her.

I go back to our table for Carol Lee, but she isn't there. Jo Anne and Andy are still at our table, and Jo Anne asks me how to get to Penn State from where we where. (We had to be somewhere near the Washington

DC or Baltimore area.) She also says they want to stop at Gettysburg on the way to Penn State. I tell her to take the Interstate north to Fredrick, Maryland. Just north of Fredrick, they would see signs to Gettysburg. Then continuing north to Harrisburg, they could take a road north, alongside the Susquehanna River and then on to Penn State.

(I had just taken this route in the month of May after Carol Lee had "passed on." I was coming from a friend's birthday party near Culpepper, Virginia, and headed north to Fredrick, Gettysburg, and then Harrisburg. However, instead of heading north to Penn State from Harrisburg, I headed east to Interstate 81 and then north to my hometown of Brandonville. Of course, I could not just pass through Gettysburg without stopping. So I stopped and toured the battlefields once again. I also took the opportunity to tour the new information center which had just opened. Our Rotary is going back to Gettysburg for our conference next year. Once more, I'll be portraying Confederate Lewis Addison Armistead and wearing the Confederate uniform Carol Lee had made for me. Being that it was near Memorial Day while I was in Brandonville, actually it was the main reason I went this way. I visited and put flowers on Carol Lee's graveside.)

I want to get back to Mae and Cliff's table, so I tell Mom and Dad that as soon as Carol Lee comes back, they should bring her over to us on the other side of the room. I know she would be very happy to see Mae again.

I wake up.

The Kehleys—Mae and Cliff, Jo Anne and Andy, Buddy and Helen, Lois and Joe, Jackie, Sonny, Billy, Tommy and Bobby—were Carol Lee and my family when we lived in Brooklyn and Staten Island. We had many happy times there and many parties.

Dream # 49

TREASURES IN HEAVEN

August 8, 2009—2:00 AM

Carol Lee and I have just returned home from a trip and have gone to bed. We are extremely tired from the trip and fall into a deep sleep.

(In the dream), I wake up the next morning and go outside to an extremely shocking sight. During the night, our two neighbors' homes had burnt entirely down to their cement bases. Absolutely nothing is left standing. Another neighbor comes out and I ask him what had happened. He says there was a big fire last night; we had slept through the entire event. Looking down the street I see a third neighbor's home. It had burnt halfway to its cement base and is still burning.

I go back into the house and my father, Ed Sr., is there with Carol Lee. I ask him if he had told Carol Lee what had happened last night. He says no. So I tell Carol Lee that two of our neighbors' homes had burnt down and that another neighbor's home is still burning. I tell her that I had looked back at our home and saw what the intense heat had done to the sides of our home, but that there is no real damage.

She begins to cry. She feels so badly for our neighbors. (We had always been very close to them.)

I wake up.

EDWARD J. SEKULA, JR.

My interpretation of the dream comes from the Bible: Mathew 6:19-21, "Do not store up riches for yourselves here on earth, . . . instead store up for yourselves riches in heaven . . . for your heart will always be where your riches are." Treasures in heaven.

The only similar experience we had was several years ago. I had just left Carol Lee at home. Pat, Dennis, and I were on our way to David's home for our annual fishing trip to Maine. We hit a very severe storm in Connecticut. A tree had fallen across Interstate 84, and we could only get around it by driving over the top branches of the tree. This meant crossing over into the opposite lane of traffic.

What I didn't know until later was that Carol Lee experienced the same severe storm in New Jersey. Only there it touched down as a small tornado. It came within one hundred yards of our home. Ten trees, including an eighty foot high oak, were toppled on our backyard. The top branches of two of them landed within ten feet of our back door. The only damage to our home was caused when they fell across our clothes line which was attached to the frame of our back door. The weight of the trees across the clothesline ripped the frame to which the line was attached from our home, but there was no other damage.

The eighty-foot oak tree landed within twenty feet of my neighbor's back porch, but did no damage.

Another interpretation of the dream is that God in his mercy often protects us from the worst that can happen. In Carol Lee and our neighbor's case, the trees could have fallen on our homes and destroyed them.

Dream # 50

A Walk in Heaven

September 23, 2009—6:00 AM

Carol Lee and I are staying in a place I cannot recognize. Someone comes to the door and tells us he has been assigned to show us around the area. He is dressed in an all-white shirt and pants. I think that maybe he is a sailor.

Carol Lee and I put on our coats. We are dressed in our finest clothes. As we start down the stairs, our dog, Buttons, comes running to us. We ask if we can take Buttons with us on our walk. Our guide says yes.

Buttons is running up and down the stairs, very excited to be going with us. Carol Lee suggests that I put Buttons on a leash so that she can't run away in the new place with which we are not familiar. I get Button's leash and try to put it on her. As I uncoil the leash and look for the snap to fasten to her collar, I notice that it is not a regular snap. At the end of the leash is a piece of leather with holes in it. I place the piece of leather around Button's collar and try to align the holes with the studs which go into the holes.

Carol Lee helps me to press them down and lock them in place.

Buttons runs ahead of us down the stairs to the door. We both notice that her hair is almost all black. It should have been black and white.

The guide opens the door, and we begin to walk outside.

I wake up.

I could easily interpret this dream as being Carol Lee, Buttons, and me arriving and being together again in heaven. The guide is not a sailor, but an angel who is taking us for a walk around heaven.

You be the judge.

Dream # 51

THE BEAUTY OF GOD'S CREATION

October 6. 2009—5:00 AM

I'm driving down the road going home. (I've been somewhere, but the dream didn't reveal where.) All of a sudden, I notice the most beautiful flower garden I had ever seen. It covers the whole hillside. There are flowers of every size and shape, yet I don't recognize even one of them. The vivid colors of the flowers run the full range of the color spectrum. The most notable of the flowers are the reds, pinks, and whites.

The only thought in my mind was that as soon as I get home, I would have to find a time when I could bring Carol Lee to see this beautiful flower garden.

I didn't wake up as I usually did, but fell into a deeper peaceful sleep.

On October 2-4, we held our Patriots' Path Council 100th year of Boy Scouting Anniversary Jamboree. It was an awesome event attended by over five thousand scouts and leaders. At one point, my friend and long-time scouter Bill Levens and me were taking a break. We were sitting on a bench in front of the administration building. Combined, we have over eighty years of scouting experience as leaders in the scouting program. We were talking about our trips to Canada and how throughout Canada you see beautiful flower gardens. I commented that, at the time,

EDWARD J. SEKULA, JR.

it was my understanding that the students who graduated from Canada's colleges with a degree in horticulture gave two years of their lives immediately after graduating to creating and maintaining these flower gardens throughout all of Canada. I told Bill, "Wouldn't it be wonderful if we did the same here in the United States?" He agreed.

Dream # 52

THE DECK

November 5, 2009—1:00 AM

Carol Lee and I are admiring our new home. It is a very large and a very beautiful one.

Jo Anne, Billy, Sonny, and Tommy Kehley are visiting us. (Coincidentally, or maybe not so coincidentally, they had braved a winter storm to travel from Brooklyn, New York to Ringtown, Pennsylvania for Carol Lee's viewing at Stauffer Funeral Home.)

We take them on a tour of our new home. There are many rooms. When we get to the back of the house, we come to a kitchen and I comment, "We have a kitchen at both ends of the house, how convenient." Beyond the kitchen is a beautiful enclosed deck. Through the windows of the deck is a beautiful view of rolling hills and a lake.

I wake up.

I have always "dreamed" of adding a deck to our home in Netcong. Maybe someday I will. There are three types of decks I have considered:

1. A simple open deck like those at our timeshare at Split Rock, Pennsylvania.

EDWARD J. SEKULA, JR.

2. A screened-in deck like the one at Summit, Masssanutten.
3. A glass-enclosed deck like those advertised in magazines or the one we pass in Maine when we are going fishing at Big Lake.

The deck in my dream above was the glass-enclosed deck.

Dream # 53

CHECKING ON ME

November 21, 2009—11:00 PM

I'm dreaming that I am in bed trying to go to sleep. The light is on in the bedroom, and I can't fall asleep.

I hear someone coming into the bedroom. It is Carol Lee. She is checking up on me.

She asks me why I hadn't fallen asleep. I tell her I don't know, for some reason, I couldn't fall asleep. (Normally I fall asleep as soon as my head hits the pillow.)

I wake up.

This was another dream where I was downstairs watching TV. Without realizing it, I fall asleep, and this time, I dream of Carol Lee. It seems my guardian angel was watching over me and checking up on me. I think of how wonderful it is. She is still with me in my dreams and always will be.

Dream # 54

Maryland Crabs

December 4, 2009—6:00 am

    Carol Lee and I are at a picnic. It resembles one of our annual Fritz family reunions that are held in July. However, I don't recognize anyone there. It is a beautiful, warm, sunny day.

    The people are spread out in an area surrounded by picnic tables with a family at each one. (This is different from our Fritz family reunions where the picnic tables are usually under a pavilion in case of in-climate weather.)

    Carol Lee and I have just finished eating our picnic meal, which she had placed in our wicker picnic basket. We decided to visit the other families.

    Suddenly, instead of walking, we are on Carol Lee's scooter. She is driving, and I am standing on the back. She drives to the picnic table at the far end of the area and stops beside the table. We realize that she had driven into an area behind the picnic table that had been roped off. The family members are selling vegetables and canned goods from that side of the table. We are in the middle of the area where they are collecting money for the food that they had sold. On one end of the table are all types of canned foods in jars. Carol Lee goes over to see what they had to sell. In another area on the table, they have corn and other

DREAMS OF CAROL LEE

fresh vegetables, and I go there. As I am getting near the section with the vegetables, I notice that people have purchased some very nice corn and decide to buy some. When I got to the corn, all that is left are ears of corn with very big kernels and were "mealy" looking. So I don't buy any. The other vegetables are the same. The best had already been sold.

As I am walking back to the scooter to wait for Carol Lee, I notice a table with "Maryland Crabs" on it. These are one of my favorite foods. I begin eating one of the crabs. I figure I would pay later for the ones I had eaten since I don't know how many I would eat. I had just taken a leg with the back fin meat on it and had put it in my mouth, when Carol Lee returned. She has an armful of jars with canned food in them. One of the jars contains "chow chow," a mixture of lima beans, corn, and cabbage. Dangling from her hand is the largest Maryland crab I had ever seen. She held of it by its claw. I take the crab from her, planning to eat it next.

I wake up.

At Thanksgiving in Maryland a little over a week ago, I mentioned to Ken that I had not gotten down for a visit when we could have Maryland crabs. This was the first time I missed coming down for crabs since I had met Carol Lee. At least once a year, we would go down to Liz and Ken's in Maryland just so we could eat Maryland crabs. I even went last year, 2008, the first year after Carol Lee had passed on, but not this year. I promised myself that next year, I would go down to Liz and Ken's just for Maryland Crabs.

Currently, this was only my second dream with Carol Lee's scooter in it. More curiously, yesterday I had just finished typing Dream # 44, "Travel Adventure," which was my first dream about her and her scooter.

Dream # 55

FIRE

January 11, 2010—6:00 AM

I'm in the kitchen of our home. For some reason, I take bills from the kitchen table, put them in a waste paper basket, and set them on fire. I'm burning them one at a time to keep the flame down. I'm watching the bright flame rise from the basket.

Suddenly, I hear Carol Lee coming down the hallway. I take the last group of bills, about six of them, and throw them on the fire. I'm hoping they will burn up before Carol Lee gets into the kitchen. They don't, and they are still burning when Carol Lee comes into the kitchen.

Instead of yelling at me for starting a fire in a waste paper basket in the kitchen, she offers me several cardboard boxes to burn. I tell her that instead of burning them, we should recycle them. She agrees.

I wake up.

For the last week, I have been collecting bills on our kitchen table. I will have to make copies of some of them to take with us (Liz and Ken) and mail them while on vacation in Florida for the next month. With only two days before our departure, I'm still not sure which ones I will have to copy. I have to wait for today's mail and then make a determination.

Last year, even though I thought I mailed them in sufficient time from Florida, two credit card companies claimed the payments were received two days after their due date, and they charged me a late fee on my next account statement. I was able to get one of the credit card companies to reverse the late charge fee. The other company not only refused to reverse the late charge, but used it as a basis for increasing the interest charged on my account to an exorbitant 26 percent. The stupidity of this credit card company in taking such action resulted in my paying off the entire account balance and never using it again. They lost a valued customer of over twenty years. How foolish.

Dream # 56

ANGER

January 14, 2010—4:00 AM

For some unknown reason, Carol Lee and I are having an argument. She won't listen to what I am saying, and I am getting angry with her. I start yelling at her, but still she will not listen to me. I grab her and start shaking her (this is something I had never done with Carol Lee), but to no avail.

Suddenly, Carol Lee slips out of my hold and falls to the floor. There are many people standing around and looking at me in disbelief of what I had just done. Their piercing looks penetrate me with their disapproval.

I become very, very sorry for my anger. A deep remorse sets in for the way I had treated Carol Lee.

I wake up.

In our entire marriage, I had never gotten this angry with Carol Lee. We were always able to talk things out and make up almost immediately. The closest I ever came to this degree of anger was the night before she "passed on." It was in fact the very last discussion we would ever have. I was trying to get her to eat a little bit of her evening meal, but she insisted that she wasn't hungry and refused to eat anything. I told her she needed to eat to keep up her strength, but she wouldn't listen. I got so angry; I told her I might as well leave and go home. I wasn't helping her, but even that didn't work.

I didn't leave, and my anger immediately subsided. I quit trying to cajole her into eating.

That evening, just after I did leave, Carol Lee had a major relapse. She refused to be taken to the ICU for intubations. The next day, she "passed on" into God's hands.

Dream # 57

THE SICKLY DUCK

January 14, 2010—5:00 AM

Carol Lee and I are in the kitchen. She is cooking. She is cutting up vegetables for our meal.

On the floor of the kitchen is a duck. It looks sickly. It is lying on the floor, hardly moving.

Carol Lee takes the knife she is cutting vegetables with and taps the duck's bill. She tells it, "You've got to eat something," but the duck still hardly moves. She taps its bill again, but this time the duck's bill falls off, and she realizes the duck will never eat again.

She picks the duck up in her arms and cuddles it. She knows it is suffering terribly. Suddenly, she takes the knife and stabs the duck, ending its suffering.

I look at Carol Lee and tell her, "That is the most humane thing I have ever seen you do."

I wake up.

This is the first time I have had two complete dreams that close together: 4:00 AM and 5:00 AM. The second dream counterbalances the first. The love and humane actions shown to the duck in the second dream counterbalances the anger in the first dream, yet they seem to be related.

As explained in the first dream, my anger was based on the fact that Carol Lee wouldn't eat—the reason being more that she couldn't without great difficulty. She would have to sit up which took more strength than she had and then try to maneuver her arms through the maze of tubes and monitors in order to remove her oxygen mask.

In a way, she was reminiscent of the "sickly duck" without its bill

The most humane thing for her to end her suffering was for God to take her into his hands.

Dream # 58

CONSOLING CAROL LEE—I

January 17, 2010—4:00 AM

Carol Lee and I were lying in bed, sleeping. I wake up (in the dream) and look into her face. I see that she is also awake, but she is crying.

I ask her, "What is the matter?" She doesn't answer. Her crying becomes more intense.

I roll over to her, kiss her, and put my arms around her. Finally, her crying subsides.

I wake up.

Even knowing that the end was near, Carol Lee never cried. She was one of the strongest persons I had ever known. When her doctor told us that her status had deteriorated to the point where the chemo was no longer effective and was doing as much damage to her body as the cancer, I was the one who lost it—crying uncontrollably.

On the way home to David's from Dartmouth Medical Center, when I turned into the road to Eastman, I again began crying uncontrollably. I could no longer drive and had to pull off the road.

It was Carol Lee who consoled me. She said, "You knew we would reach this point."

I said to myself, "The clock is ticking."

Dream # 59

CONSOLING CAROL LEE—II

January 17, 2010—5:30 AM

This is the second time I have had two consecutive dreams of Carol Lee in the same night.

This time, it was the exact same dream.

Having the exact same dream is a first for me.

The fact that this was our second night in our condo in Florida and that I missed Carol Lee so very, very much may have led to these identical dreams. I wanted her to be here with me even if I had to console her as she had consoled me so many, many times.

Maybe I wanted to return the favor even though I had actually consoled her many, many times as well.

I wanted to show her how much I appreciated her consolation.

Dream # 60

Carol Lee's "Passing On"

January 26, 2010—3:00 AM

While this was "technically" not a dream, I woke up at 3:00 AM and couldn't go back to sleep.

Yesterday, Liz, Ken, and I went to the AMC Theaters in Downtown Disney. We thought the movie we wanted to see started at 4:10, but it actually didn't start until 5:10. Instead of waiting around for it to start, we decided to see our second-choice movie. We had already planned to come later in our vacation to see it. The movie was *The Blind Side*.

It turned out to be one of the best movies we had seen in a long time.

However, at one point in the movie, I totally lost it. "Big Mike" when asked a question, answered, "I don't know." These were the last words spoken by Carol Lee. I couldn't hold back the tears, which came streaming down my face.

The second anniversary of her "passing on" was just two day away: January 27, 2010.

It took me several minutes to regain control of myself by getting back into the progress of the movie.

EDWARD J. SEKULA, JR.

Again, later in the movie, Big Mike's mother, when asked a question, replied, "I don't know." Again, I lost it. After a few minutes, I was able to get back into the movie and regain my composure.

While I had just awakened and was trying to get back to sleep, a state of semiconsciousness, my mind flashed back to the movie and Carol Lee's last words.

On the day that she "passed on," I listened to my telephone messages after coming home from worship services at Abiding Peace Lutheran Church—one from her doctor and two from her nurse. I immediately knew, "This is it."

I hurriedly drove to Morristown Memorial Hospital and ran to Carol Lee's bedside. She was in the room by herself. Neither her nurse or her doctor who had called me were around to tell me what had happened.

One glance at Carol Lee's monitor near her bedside told me everything. All readings were at the critical stage. Except for the monitor's connection and an IV administering her pain medication, all the other connections including her oxygen tubing had been removed. This truly was "it."

I walked up to Carol Lee's bedside, kissed her on the cheek, and placed my hand on her forehead, I asked her, "What happened to you?" Not expecting an answer. Her eyes had been closed, and I didn't expect her to open them. But to my surprise, she turned her head toward me, opened her eyes for the last time, and answered, "I don't know."

She then turned her head back to an upright position and closed her eyes.

Seven hours later, after a tremendous struggle to stay alive, I squeezed her hand a little harder and said to her, "Its OK! Let go! Go to God!" And immediately she "passed on" into God's hands.

Dream # 61

BEING SAVED

January 26, 2010

Usually, when I wake up and record one of my dreams, I can return to bed and immediately go back to sleep. Instead of falling asleep, my mind kept telling me that I hadn't gone far enough in recording my thoughts on "passing on."

As I expressed previously, my dreams of Carol Lee early in our marriage where she "passes on" in a fire and where God had revealed to me that her name was recorded in the "Book of Life" assured me that Carol Lee would be saved and have eternal life.

However, the dream also created the greatest fear—what if I were not saved?

Having been baptized in the Roman Catholic Church, but brought up in the Evangelical Lutheran Church, I strived to become more involved in my church. The dream encouraged me to become even more involved.

Carol Lee's illness and the time I spent by her bedside allowed me to reread the Bible several times. It also allowed me to read the books not included in the Bible.

EDWARD J. SEKULA, JR.

Her passing on encouraged me to go even deeper in my reading. My original fear was now heightened. The spark of life (soul, spirit) given by God to Carol Lee at her birth has now gone back to God. And she is now in his presence.

How do I assure that once the "spark" of my life given by God at my birth will return to him and reunite with Carol Lee's "spark," where together we can sing God's praises throughout all eternity?

The answer is that Jesus has already assured me that those who believe will have everlasting life. "On account of Christ," my sins are forgiven.

Recently, one of the members of my congregation asked me, "What do I have to do to be saved?" I answered, "You are already saved." I was further asked, "But what if I cross the line in what I am doing?" I answered, "On account of Christ, your sins are forgiven."
I told him that sometimes I worry about the same thing, but I know that if I cross the line,
"on account of Christ," my sins are forgiven, and God will guide me back to the right side of the line.

Since Carol Lee's passing on, I have had the opportunity to read the *Book of Concord*, which details Lutheran theology.

I have learned that we cannot be saved by our own merit or anything we do. We cannot save ourselves.

But "on account of Christ," we are already saved. All we have to do is to be assured of eternal life, to believe that Jesus, the Christ, is our Lord and Savior, and to have faith (justification by faith alone) in him and his promise of eternal life.

Until the day when the spark of life leaves my body, my goal in life is to grow in faith.

When the spark of life leaves our bodies on this planet, and we are rejoined with all the saints and heavenly hosts, as I believe mine will be with Carol Lee, we will be in the presence of God and will sing his praises throughout all eternity. Amen.

Dream # 62

Getting Home in the Dark

February 9. 1010—6:00 AM

Carol Lee and I are leaving an event we had just attended. It is very dark. We get into our car, and I start backing out of our parking spot. I turn the wheel a little too hard and tap the car beside us. As I back out, we notice a small dent in the car. Carol Lee exclaims, "You put a dent in the other car." I become concerned, but as I continue backing out, I notice other dents in the car beside us. Someone else had made all the other dents. I tell Carol Lee that the way I had tapped the other car, I should not have made a dent in it. I complete backing out and start down the road.

It is very dark with no lights beside the road. It is so dark I could hardly see the road. There is a pile of rocks in the roadway, and I am lucky to see them and drive around them.

Suddenly, I spot several deer along the side of the road. Again, it is very difficult to see the in the dark, but there is enough light from my headlights to see them. One of the deer is a little fawn. I am afraid of hitting one of the deer, so I slow down. There are more deer on the other side of the road, and I very slowly drive between them.

I don't know where we are. Soon, we come to some buildings, a group of cabins on both sides of the road. I drive between them and suddenly the road ends. I say there must have been a turn in the road before we got to the cabins. I back up and sure enough there is a turn in the road.

I turn onto the road, and we are again on our way home.

I wake up.

In real life, I had two similar experiences. One with Carol Lee where we had come to a stop sign where the road ended and you had to turn left or right. We didn't want to go either left or right, so I began backing up. The road was clear behind me, but another car turned onto the road right behind me and didn't see that I was backing up (my backup lights were on). Obviously, I backed into the car causing damage to the other car's bumper, but none to ours.

The second similar event was after Carol Lee had passed on. It was a Shop Rite parking lot, and I was backing out of my parking spot. I looked behind me, and saw that it was clear. However, as I started backing up, another car stopped directly behind me, and I didn't see it. Obviously, I backed into the car creating a very small dent in the car's door.

These may or may not have caused the dream.

Dream # 63

GETTING BACK TO CAROL LEE

February 10, 2010—3:30 AM

Carol Lee and I are on a "road trip" in our second old car (I don't know which one). We are traveling through an unfamiliar area. Suddenly, our car stops running. I let it coast to the side of the road. We get out of the car. I don't know what to do.

Carol Lee tells me to go back home and get our Mercury Marquis. So I begin walking back toward our home. Someone gives me a ride, but we begin traveling in the wrong direction. The driver and his wife are going to see the local sites. We come to a mountain and stop.
It is one of the most beautiful sites I have ever seen. The mountains seem to stretch forever.
We could not see the other side or the end of them, yet I know Carol Lee was on the other side of them. I could not believe we had traveled so far from her. We finally come down from the mountain top, get back in the car and again begin traveling toward home.

I get into our new Mercury Marquis and begin traveling back toward Carol Lee. I suddenly realize I don't know where I had left her. I don't know which road to take. I don't know the closest town to her. I have no way of contacting her. How do I find her?

DREAMS OF CAROL LEE

I know we had traveled west, so I begin driving in that direction. I stop for something to eat.

In the side room of the restaurant, there is a party going on. They are eating and drinking and singing karaoke. They ask me to join them. So I did. I lose track of time.

Realizing it is late, I excuse myself and begin to leave.

As I am getting into the car, I recognize an old couple and say hello to them. I become very embarrassed. I am here partying while poor Carol Lee is sitting at the roadside somewhere west of me.

I begin driving and look at the clock on the dash. It is six o'clock. I left Carol Lee at the the roadside at one o'clock—five hours ago. How could I justify taking all that time while she is sitting there all alone just waiting for me to come back and take her home?

Once again, I realize I don't know where she is. How will I find her? Our GPS (we didn't have GPS on our cars; it wasn't invented yet. This past Christmas, our son, David, got one for my van) is in the other car that had broken down with Carol Lee staying near it. Even if I do have the GPS, I don't know the town or address.

I realize then that there was no way I could get back to her. I begin wondering what she would do. She has no way to contact me.

I wake up.

Carol Lee's passing on was like this dream. She had left me and gone into "God's hands."

My recent study of the *Book of Concord* tells me there is no way I can get to heaven, back to Carol Lee, by my own efforts. The only way to get back to her, to be reunited with her, is through the promise of our Lord and Savior, Jesus the Christ. We are "justified by faith alone." All we have to do is believe in him. Jesus said,

He who believes in me shall never die.
For God so loved the world so much that he gave his only Son so that everyone who believes in him may not die but have eternal life.

I need only believe and work to strengthen my faith until the day I too will pass on into God's hands and be in his presence. Then and only then can I rejoin Carol Lee in heaven. Amen.

Dream # 64

SPARKS

March 29, 2010—2:00 AM

Carol Lee is sitting at her sewing machine sewing something. I am standing there watching her.

Suddenly, sparks start flying from the electric cord attached to her sewing machine. I tell her to turn the machine off. She stops sewing.

I examine the cord and see that several of the wires have been exposed and are touching one another. When they touch together, the sparks go flying.

I look back at Carol Lee. She has wrapped herself in a quilt. I ask her, "What is the matter? She says she is very cold.

I wake up.

This is the first dream I have had about Carol Lee since my return from my Florida vacation.

When Carol Lee's cancer had progressed to the point that her hands would no longer allow her to operate her sewing machine, she became aware that this was the first of many things that she enjoyed, that she could no longer do. Some would call this "portends of the future." Such a thought would certainly make anyone cold.

It would also remind them of the inevitable, the loss of one's "spark of life" here on earth.

However, with the hope and assurance of the resurrection, as promised by Jesus, we know that our spark of life will return to God as Carol Lee's most certainly has.

Dream # 65

THE LOST SCOUT PATROL

April 25, 2010—2:10 AM

I am asleep in a cabin at a scout camp. Carol Lee is with me in bed in the cabin.

(In real life, she had never gone camping with me at a scout camp.) Our son, David, is also camping with us.

In the middle of the night, Carol Lee wakes me up. She tells me David has not returned from a hiking trip. I become very concerned that he might have become lost. We get up, get dressed, and go outside. I yell, "David, David." We hear a faint voice in the distance.

I tell Carol Lee, "Let's go to the car." He will be able to hear our car's horn better than our voices and follow the sound back to us. So we rush to our car. I open the door and give the horn several long blasts. I don't care that I might waken the whole camp. We get out of the car to listen for a response from David, but we don't hear anything. I plan to wait a short time and then repeat the blasts on the horn. I just know he would be able to follow the sound back to the car.

As I was about to sound the horn again, Carol Lee yells, "There he is." David comes up the hill to where our car is parked. He is followed by a group of young scouts. They are all dressed in their class A uniforms. They are all happy to get back to camp and are in good spirits.

I ask David if any of the scouts had been hurt, and he answers no. The scouts seem to enjoy the challenge of being lost and finding their way home. This is an experience they would all long remember. I ask David how many scouts he has in the patrol. He answers, "Ten." All ten are accounted for.

Carol Lee is happy that David has found his way back to camp with all of the scouts.
She goes back to the cabin to go back to sleep.

I tell David I would go to camp headquarters with him. I am sure the scoutmasters had reported their missing scouts and that David would take some "heat" for getting them lost. As we walk down the trail to the headquarters building, David tells me that even though he didn't know the camp area where they were hiking, he accepted the responsibility for leading the hike because no other leaders would step forward.

While I was concerned when Carol Lee and I realized that he had gotten lost, I wasn't that worried. I know that David could handle almost any situation.

I wake up.

In real life, David and I had encountered this situation too many times. Not just in scouting but in all aspects of life. Because no one else would step forward and volunteer to do something, we had to accept the responsibility and risk of volunteering ourselves. We did it for the sake of those who would benefit from our doing it. Even in retirement, I find myself taking on more responsibility than I can handle, simply because no one else will volunteer. I wish there were more volunteers to do the things that need to be done.

Even in my church where I serve as chairman of our evangelism committee, I wish there were more volunteers to do the work God has called us to do. I wish there were more people to spread the "Good News" of Jesus in the communities in which we live.

This past week, a scout came to me for his fishing merit badge award for which I am a counselor. He was dressed in his class "A" uniform and had his merit badge sash containing all the merit badges he had earned over his shoulder. Judging by the number of merit badges on the sash, it was obvious that he was close to earning the honor of becoming an Eagle Scout. It has always given me great pride to know I helped a scout on his "Trail of Eagle—to become an Eagle Scout. One of Carol Lee's greatest prides was when David had received his Eagle Scout award.

Possibly, the event of the scout coming to me for his fishing merit badge triggered this dream; possibly not?

Dream # 66

WORSHIP SERVICE AT ST. JOHN'S LUTHERAN CHURCH

Brandonville
September 17, 2010—4:00 AM

Carol Lee and I are attending worship service at St. John's Lutheran Church in Brandonville, Pennsylvania—my home congregation. We are sitting in the pew on the left-hand side of the worship area. This is the same pew that my mother, Dorothy Sekula, and I sat when we attended worship. It is also the same pew that Carol Lee and I sat when attending service and the same pew that I sit in since Carol Lee passed on.

In the middle of the liturgy, we begin a responsive reading that I am not familiar with. I begin searching the service setting in my hymnal to find where we are, but I can't find it. I look at Carol Lee, and she shows me an insert that somehow I did not get. There are several words written on the insert that I am not familiar with, either Greek or Latin. (While I saw the entire word on the insert in my dream, I could only remember the first few letters: Elio . . . and Kio . . .).

After the service, Carol Lee walks out the building with the other parishioners. Oddly, though I'm related to most of them, I don't recognize anyone. Carol Lee spots someone off to the side and goes over to talk with her. I don't recognize the person she is talking with.

Suddenly, I find myself beside and talking with my pastor at Abiding Peace Lutheran Church in Budd Lake. She is saying how great it is to have a larger than usual attendance at the service. I agree with her and say how great it is to see such a large attendance.

Carol Lee finishes talking with the person I don't know and joins a group of other parishioners, again none of which I recognize. She starts walking away with them, and suddenly, I realize I couldn't go with them. Suddenly, I am walking all by myself, and I feel very lonely.

I wake up.

*　　*　　*

On Sunday, September 5, while attending our thirty-first Sekula family reunion, I visited Carol Lee's graveside in the cemetery beside St. John's and attended worship service, sitting in the same pew in which we had always sat. This past week, Tuesday, September 14, I attended our evangelism team meeting at Abiding Peace Lutheran Church in Budd Lake with our pastor Becky Thane. These events may have led to the dream.

My interpretation of the essence of the dream was that Carol Lee and I were attending a service in heaven. This is why I didn't recognize anyone other than Carol Lee and Pastor Thane. This is the reason she went with the other parishioners, and I couldn't go with them—yet. Pastor and I were discussing evangelism and our hope that we can reach out into the community so that others can hear and receive the message of the Good News of Jesus Christ. The increase in attendance at Abiding Peace relates to the happiness both of us felt at the increase in worship attendance. We prayed for that at the conclusion of our meeting. I continue to pray daily for our outreach into our communities.

Carol Lee: Postscript

(Gateway to Heaven)

In addition to rendering Carol Lee's eulogy at both her funeral service at St. John's Lutheran Church in Brandonville, Pennsylvania, and her memorial service at Abiding Peace Lutheran Church in Budd Lake, I also delivered a "postscript."

The basis for her eulogy came to me at 4:00 AM on January 29, the third night after her "passing on." While lying in bed, the thoughts came to me, and I concluded that I should be the one to deliver her eulogy. I immediately got up and recorded my thoughts. They forever will be my tribute to her memory.

The next night, January 30, 2008, was my first visit from Carol Lee from heaven.
After this first dream, I immediately woke up, went to our kitchen, and recorded the dream. It was a very special message from her and one that I continue to follow.

I decided to include her revelation as a postscript to her eulogy.

EDWARD J. SEKULA, JR.

"Gateway to Heaven"

I was only going to share this with my immediate family, but you are all my family and friends. For any who doubt the existence of heaven, be assured that there truly is a heaven. I have been blessed with the ability to dream in vivid color. I have also been blessed with almost total recall of many of my dreams. Often my parents, Ed Sr. and Dorothy, visit me from heaven, and we go fishing together. Often my cousin John visits me, and we go fishing.

Carol Lee has already visited me from heaven in a dream. She is now my guardian angel. She revealed to me that I would have a rich new life, but the beginning would be very difficult. She assured me that even strangers would help me. She cautioned me to go slow. Most importantly, she revealed to me that she was waiting for me to return to her at the "gateway to heaven."

Prayer:

Heavenly Father, Lord Jesus, Holy Spirit,

Thank you for allowing me to share my life with Carol Lee.

Amen.

Gate to Heaven: (Mathew 7:13-14)

Go through the narrow gate because the gate to hell is wide and the road that to it is easy, and there are many who travel it. But the gate to life is narrow and the way that leads to it is hard, and there are few people who find it.

Carol Lee found it, and it is my sincere prayer and hope that I too shall find it and join her in the presence of God (heaven). May our "sparks of life" once more be reunited. Amen.

DREAMS OF CAROL LEE

In a pamphlet supplied by the Edmundite Missions, Selma Alabama, they define *angels*. "Angels are spiritual beings who are constantly in God's presence, singing praises to him, our Creator. Angels serve as divine messengers, bringing God's will and word to men and women. Angels serve as our appointed guardians, protecting and watching over us at God's command."

Carol Lee is now my guardian angel, who now visits me in my dreams. I firmly believe that someday I will join her in the presence of God, and together, we will sing praises to him throughout all eternity. Amen.

In a sense, the "gateway to heaven" physically exists, at least in my mind. On the summer before her passing on, Carol Lee and I along with our son, David, and his family were vacationing at our timeshare at Massanutten, Virginia. We had taken the ski lift to the top which is near the southern tip of the Massanutten Mountains. From the peak, a path leads down to an outcropping of rock called "Lookout Point." It was the spot where the Confederate general Stonewall Jackson had posted his signal officer. The signal officer advised General Jackson of the status of the two Union Armies approaching him from both sides of the Massanutten Mountain. This information was key to Jackson's defeating one Union Army at Cross Keys on one day and the other Union Army the next day at Port Republic.

I didn't go down the path to the lookout point. I did it the next year after Carol Lee had passed on. When I did go down to the point the next year, I was astonished to find that they had built a platform over the rock outcrop. At the end was a gate. Sky divers would open the gate and jump off. They could then sail south to the battlefields—west to Harrisonburg and James Madison University (where Carol Lee's sister Liz's two daughters graduated from college) or north up either side of the Shenandoah Valley.

The platform and gateway were exactly the way they looked in the dream; they were actually real although I had not seen them until after the dream.

Edwards Brothers,Inc!
Thorofare, NJ 08086
13 April, 2011
BA2011103